Welcome

A Training Course of the National Safety Council

The National Safety Council is America's leading nonprofit safety advocate – and has been for over 100 years. As a mission-based organization, we focus on eliminating the leading causes of preventable death so people can live their fullest lives. We focus our efforts where we can make the greatest impact: workplace, roadway and impairment.

NSC starts at work – where people put everyday strategies in place to solve problems. We give companies resources workers can actually use around risks they are actually facing, or will be. We create a culture of safety to not only make people safer at work but also because it has the potential to make people safer beyond the workplace. Research shows safer workplaces save money and increase productivity, but more importantly, they create a mindset that values safety.

NSC has a long history of convening with its unparalleled network of safety leaders to make people's lives safer on and off the job. We tap the expertise, talent and passion of our network to develop research and ready-to-use toolkits to help companies tackle important issues affecting their workers. Every one of our employees, member organizations and strategic partners have one thing in common: a commitment to enable people to live their fullest lives.

NSC uses research and data to drive better, smarter, more personal safety programs. From perception surveys and assessments to tracking the trends, we use our insight to create real, usable, experiential education, training and tools to mitigate risk. We also engage government across national and local levels to advocate for awareness and drive polices that create a culture of safety.

Save lives, from the workplace to anyplace.™

NSC Bloodborne & Airborne Pathogens

Table of Contents

Module 1 Introduction to the Bloodborne Pathogens Standard 1

Module 2 Bloodborne Pathogens 5

Module 3 Preventing Infection from Bloodborne Pathogens 18

Module 4 Airborne Pathogens 37

Sample Forms 49

Index. 60

Introduction to the Bloodborne Pathogens Standard

Module Objectives

By the end of this module, you will be able to:

- Describe the purpose of the OSHA Bloodborne Pathogens Standard.
- Define who the Standard protects.
- List examples of employees covered by the Standard.
- Describe the general goals of required bloodborne pathogens training.

Video Review

1. How are bloodborne pathogens transmitted from one person to another?

_____

2. How are airborne pathogens transmitted from one person to another?

_____

The United States Occupational Safety and Health Administration (OSHA) creates and enforces safety standards for workplaces. The Occupational Exposure to Bloodborne Pathogens Standard (the Standard) was designed to eliminate or minimize employees' exposure to human blood and other potentially infectious materials (OPIM) in the workplace. The Standard went into effect in 1992 and applies to all employees who, as part of their job, may reasonably expect to be exposed to blood and OPIM that may contain pathogens.

Overview

Pathogens are germs that cause disease. Bloodborne pathogens are germs transmitted from one person to another through contact with blood or OPIM. OPIM include human body fluids and anything contaminated by them. Module 2 contains a listing of body fluids that are potentially infectious. The Standard applies to employees who may be at risk even if their jobs for the most part do not involve giving first aid or working near or with bloodborne pathogens (Figure 1-1).

The United States Centers for Disease Control and Prevention (CDC) also provides guidelines for preventing exposure to bloodborne pathogens. Practices and procedures from both organizations are included in this guide.

Practices described in this guide also meet the required education and training standards of the National Fire Protection Association (NFPA) for infection control. Additional recommendations for infection control programs for fire departments can be found in NFPA 1581(http://www.nfpa.org).

Figure 1-1 *The OSHA Bloodborne Standard protects employees in many different occupations.*

Who Does the Standard Protect?

The Standard protects full-time, part-time and temporary employees whose job involves handling or possibly being exposed to blood or blood products, blood components or OPIM. This includes but is not limited to:

- Airline mechanics
- Animal handlers
- Athletic trainers
- Clinical technicians
- Correctional officers
- Custodians
- Dentists and other dental workers
- EMS providers (**Figure 1-2**)
- Engineering staff
- Firefighters
- Health care workers
- Housekeeping personnel
- Hospice employees
- Law enforcement personnel
- Lifeguards
- Massage therapists
- Modification practitioners (tattoo and body piercing artists)
- Morticians
- Physical therapists
- Research technicians
- Veterinarians
- Waste collectors

OSHA estimates that millions of workers in health care and related occupations are at risk for occupational exposure to bloodborne pathogens. The CDC estimates that more than 3.25 million people in the United States population, are living with chronic hepatitis B virus (HBV) or hepatitis C virus (HCV) infections.

You do not need to directly contact someone carrying a bloodborne pathogen to be at risk for exposure. Employees who perform job tasks such as handling clinical specimens, biohazardous trash, blood or body-fluid-soaked

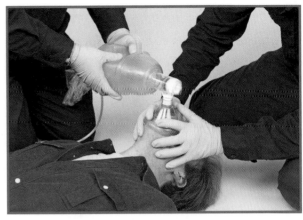

Figure 1-2 *EMS workers are covered by the Standard.*

laundry or needles or other sharps should also have bloodborne pathogens training. It is the employer's responsibility to determine which job classifications or specific tasks and procedures involve occupational exposure.

Who Is Excluded from the Standard?

The construction industry is not covered by the Standard. However, OSHA's General Duty Clause (Section 5(a) (1)) is used to protect employees from bloodborne pathogens in construction.

The Standard does not cover people who give first aid as Good Samaritans. This is first aid a person voluntarily gives to another person, such as performing CPR or helping someone with a cut, nose bleed or other injury off the job. The Standard focuses on occupational exposure, which is specifically defined by OSHA as "a reasonably anticipated skin, eye, mucous membrane or parenteral contact with blood or OPIM that may result from the performance of employees' duties."

What Training Is Required?

The Standard requires that all employees who perform tasks involving potential occupational exposure to bloodborne pathogens receive initial and annual training. Initial training must be conducted prior to being placed in positions where occupational exposure may occur. Employees must be retrained at least once every 12 months (within a time period not to exceed 365 days), regardless of the employee's other training or education. Circumstances that warrant more frequent training may occur (e.g., when there are changes in workplace practices, procedures or tasks or when employee performance suggests the prior training was incomplete or not fully understood).

The training should cover the hazards employees face (how bloodborne diseases are transmitted and their symptoms), the protective measures they can take to prevent exposure and procedures to follow if they are exposed. Industry-specific and site-specific information must be included.

Employers should tailor the training to the employee's background and responsibilities.

What Else Is Required by the Standard?

The Standard requires that, where appropriate, employers have a written Exposure Control Plan that clearly outlines how employees are to prevent exposures through engineering controls, work practice controls, universal precautions and personal protective equipment. The Plan must be accessible to employees as well as to OSHA and NIOSH representatives. These topics are covered in detail later in this guide.

The Standard also requires recordkeeping. Recordkeeping for exposure incidents must comply with OSHA 29 CFR Part 1904 ("Occupational Injury and Illness Recording and Reporting Requirements") or applicable State plan provisions, using OSHA Form 300 (**Figure 1-3**) and

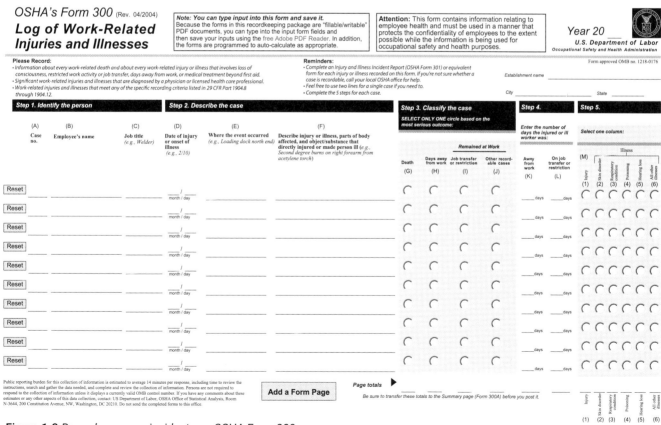

Figure 1-3 *Record exposure incidents on OSHA Form 300.*

either OSHA Form 301 or the incident reporting form used by the organization. Records must be kept in accordance with the Health Insurance Portability and Accountability Act (HIPAA) and must be maintained for a minimum of 5 years. Copies of these forms can be obtained on OSHA's website at www.osha.gov.

Training records must be kept for 3 years from the date of training and should include the dates of the training sessions, the contents or a summary of the training, the names and qualifications of the people conducting the training and the names and job titles of all who attended the training session. A sample bloodborne pathogens training log is included in the back of this Participant Guide.

Other Regulations

The Needlestick Safety and Prevention Act, which became effective in April 2001, requires employers to identify, evaluate and implement safer medical devices. The Act provides expanded protection for employees, including maintaining a sharps injury log that serves as a tool for identifying high-risk areas and

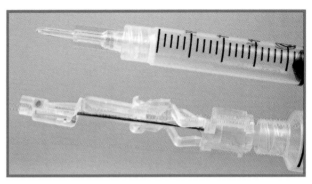

Figure 1-4 *To reduce the risk of accidental needlesticks from conventional syringes with needles, many employers are now using needleless devices and self-sheathing needles.*

evaluating devices. Employers are required to review the log both periodically and as part of the annual review and update of the Exposure Control Plan. Employers also are required to annually document their consideration and implementation of appropriate commercially available and effective safer medical devices and to involve non-management workers in evaluating and choosing them (**Figure 1-4**). Employers are given flexibility to solicit employee input in a manner appropriate to the circumstances of the workplace.

Learning Checkpoint 1

1. The OSHA Bloodborne Pathogens Standard covers all employees who, in the course of their daily work, may reasonably expect to be exposed to blood or OPIM that may contain bloodborne pathogens. **True**   **False**

2. Only health care workers are covered under the Bloodborne Pathogens Standard. **True**   **False**

3. A Good Samaritan is –
   a. always covered by the Bloodborne Pathogens Standard.
   b. not covered by the Bloodborne Pathogens Standard.
   c. covered only when helping a coworker.
   d. covered only when on company property.

4. OSHA mandates that employees who may be exposed to bloodborne pathogens receive training every 5 years. **True**   **False**

Bloodborne Pathogens

2

Module Objectives

By the end of this module, you will be able to:

- Describe the stages by which infectious diseases are transmitted from one person to another.
- List body fluids that may contain bloodborne pathogens.

- For the bloodborne diseases Hepatitis B, Hepatitis C and Human Immunodeficiency Virus, describe:
  - How it is transmitted
  - Its primary symptoms
  - Whether a vaccine is available
  - How to prevent infection
  - Who should be tested

Video Review

1. For which bloodborne disease is there an effective vaccine that helps prevent infection: HBV, HCV or HIV?

An occupational exposure to infected blood or OPIM can occur in many occupations. An occupational exposure puts you at risk for infection from disease-causing microorganisms and could result in hepatitis B, hepatitis C or HIV.

How Are Infectious Diseases Transmitted?

Preventing transmission of infectious disease is based on understanding how disease is transmitted (**Figure 2-1**). This process involves 4 stages

1. *The process begins with an infected individual.*
2. *The infectious pathogen (disease-causing bacteria, virus, fungus or parasite) leaves the infected person's body.* For example:
   - The person may bleed from a cut, and in that person's blood is the pathogen.
   - The person may sneeze or cough out little droplets carrying the pathogen.
3. *The infectious pathogen reaches another person and enters his or her body.* This can happen in a number of ways:

Figure 2-1 *Different modes of disease transmission.*

- The person may come into contact with the infected person's blood, body fluid or other infectious material in a way such that the pathogen enters his or her body through mucous membranes or non-intact skin **(bloodborne transmission).**
- The person may inhale the pathogen in tiny droplets in the air **(airborne transmission).**
- The person may be bitten by an insect, such as a tick or mosquito, carrying the pathogen **(vector transmission).**

Transmission of a pathogen from one person to another is said to occur through direct or in direct contact:

- **Direct contact** occurs with contact with an infected person or fluids or substances from that person.
- **Indirect contact** occurs with contact with contaminated objects, droplets in the air or vectors such as insects.

4. ***The second person develops the infection.*** Just having the pathogen enter the body does not automatically mean a person will become ill. He or she may have been vaccinated against the disease, which helps protect the body by developing antibodies to kill or limit the pathogen's ability to cause the disease. A person's natural immune system may be able to kill some pathogens and thereby prevent illness. Or a person may become infected. The process then starts all over again.

What Are Bloodborne Pathogens?

Bloodborne pathogens are microorganisms that are present in human blood and can cause disease in humans. Common serious bloodborne pathogens that may be encountered in the workplace include, but are not limited to:

- Hepatitis B virus (HBV)
- Hepatitis C virus (HCV)
- Human immunodeficiency virus (HIV), which can lead to acquired immunodeficiency syndrome (AIDS)

Other diseases that may result from bloodborne pathogens are described at the end of this module.

Although the OSHA Occupational Exposure to Bloodborne Pathogens Standard (the Standard) covers all bloodborne pathogens, this guide describes only HBV, HCV and HIV because these are the most common and serious pathogens you will likely come in contact with at work in the United States. Measures you take to prevent these infections will also help prevent diseases caused by other bloodborne pathogens.

What Other Substances Are Potentially Infectious?

Both blood and **other potentially infectious materials (OPIM)** may contain bloodborne pathogens. According to the Standard, OPIM may include these human body fluids and anything contaminated with them:

- Saliva containing blood (as in dental procedures)
- Semen
- Vaginal secretions
- Breast milk
- Amniotic fluid (the fluid in the uterus around the fetus)
- Cerebrospinal fluid (the fluid that surrounds the spinal cord and brain)
- Synovial fluid (the fluid in joints)
- Pleural fluid (the fluid between the linings of the lungs)
- Peritoneal fluid (the fluid contained in the abdomen)
- Pericardial fluid (the fluid surrounding heart)
- Any body fluid visibly contaminated with blood (such as vomit or urine)

OPIM may also include the following **(Figure 2-2):**

- Blood, organs or other tissue from experimental animals infected with HBV or HIV
- Tissue samples or organ cultures or cell cultures containing HIV

Figure 2-2 *Potentially infectious materials include tissues and some lab animals.*

- Non-intact skin (acne, burns, rashes, etc.) or organs from a human
- HBV-containing cultures or other solutions

Do Exposures Always Cause Infection?

Exposures do not always cause infection. The risk of infection following an exposure to blood or another body fluid depends on many factors, including:

- Whether pathogens are present in the source blood or body fluid
- The number of pathogens present
- The type of injury or exposure – how the infectious material gets into your body
- Your current health and immunization status

This means even if the source person's blood or OPIM contain pathogens, you are not necessarily infected. To be safe, however, always assume an exposure is potentially infectious and follow all recommended measures to prevent exposures from occurring.

 ## Unknown Body Fluid

You must also take precautions in situations when it is not possible to identify a body fluid. Any unknown fluid suspected to be a body fluid should be handled according to OSHA standards.

 ## Learning Checkpoint 1

1. There are only 3 bloodborne pathogens: HBV, HCV and HIV.   **True**   **False**

2. Bloodborne pathogens are present in all human blood and will cause   **True**   **False**
   disease in people who have weak immune systems.

3. OPIM include: (Circle all that apply.)
   a. Saliva in dental procedures   c. Vaginal secretions
   b. Semen   d. Bloody vomit

4. What other substances can contain bloodborne pathogens?
   (Circle all that apply.)
   a. HBV-containing cultures or   c. Tissue or organ cultures or
      other solutions   cell cultures containing HIV
   b. Breast milk   d. Animal blood
        e. Vomit containing blood

Hepatitis

Hepatitis means inflammation of the liver and also refers to a group of viral infections that affect the liver. The most common types are hepatitis A, hepatitis B and hepatitis C.

Viral hepatitis is the leading cause of liver cancer and the most common reason for liver transplantation. Millions of Americans are living with chronic hepatitis, and most do not know they are infected.[1]

Hepatitis B

Hepatitis B, also called serum hepatitis, is caused by the **hepatitis B virus (HBV)** HBV is transmitted by blood and OPIM. Although HBV has been found in all body secretions and excretions, blood and semen are the most infectious. HBV infections are a major cause of liver damage, cirrhosis and liver cancer. Because of routine hepatitis B vaccinations, the number of new infections per year has declined significantly, particularly in children and adolescents. However, the Centers for Disease Control and Prevention (CDC) reports that in the United States HBV still infects more than 21,000 people yearly, and there are about 850,000 chronic carriers in the population. It is estimated that more than 1,600 people die of liver problems associated with HBV infection every year.[2]

The time from exposure to developing HBV averages 120 days, with a range of 45-160 days. Infection by HBV can cause either acute hepatitis or a chronic (long-term) HBV infection, depending on how the body responds to the virus. In most cases the body produces an antibody that helps destroy liver cells that contain the virus, which eliminates the virus from the body. The person then has lifelong immunity to the hepatitis B virus. About 95% of adults who are infected develop antibodies and recover within 6 months of being infected. Once they recover, they are not infectious to others.

Those who do develop chronic HBV infections, however, do not develop the antibody and can carry the virus and be infectious to others for decades. A person who still has the virus 6 months after infection is considered chronically infected. Chronic infection can lead to severe liver damage and death.

How Is HBV Spread?

HBV is spread in the following ways:

- By injection (such as needlesticks or puncture wounds)
- Through mucous membranes (blood contamination through the eye or mouth) and non-intact skin (for example, abrasions or lacerations)
- Through sexual activity
- From infected mother to newborn at birth

The most likely mode of transmission of HBV is direct contact with infectious blood through a needlestick or injury by another sharp instrument. Health care workers face these risks in the work environment **(Figure 2-3)**. With current blood testing, the blood supply today is generally safe, although a theoretical risk of infection remains with blood transfusions.

Exposure to HBV on contaminated environmental surfaces is another common mode of transmission. At room temperature the virus may

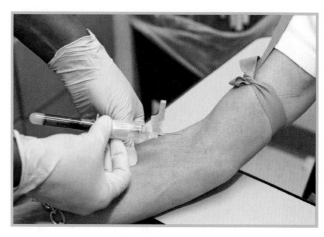

Figure 2-3 *Direct exposure to infected blood is the greatest risk for bloodborne disease.*

[1](http://www.cdc.gov/hepatitis/index.htm Accessed 09/20/21)
[2](http://www.cdc.gov/hepatitis/Resources/Professionals/PDFs/ABCTable.pdf Accessed 09/20/21)

Figure 2-4 *HBV can live for many days on contaminated surfaces.*

survive for at least 1 week in dried body fluids on surfaces such as tables and faucets (**Figure 2-4**). HBV is easily transmitted because it can live longer than other pathogens outside the body and because very little blood is needed to cause infection. HBV can be spread by sharing such personal items as a razor, toothbrush or drug paraphernalia like needles and syringes.

HBV is not transmitted in food or water, in fecal matter, through the air or through casual contact with an infected person (**Figure 2-5**). Casual contact includes activities such as the following:

• Sharing a meal, utensils or a drinking glass
• Kissing, hugging or touching

Figure 2-5 *Casual contact does not transmit HBV.*

• Being around someone who sneezes or coughs
• Sharing a phone or bathroom

Symptoms of HBV

About 30% of HBV-infected people have no symptoms. When symptoms do occur, they usually appear gradually and are often flu-like. These symptoms may include the following:

• Fever
• Fatigue
• Loss of appetite
• Nausea, vomiting
• Abdominal pain
• Dark urine
• Clay-colored stool
• Joint pain
• Jaundice

HEPATITIS B VACCINATION

In the typical vaccination schedule, the second dose is generally given 1 month after the first, and the third dose 6 months after the first.

This schedule may vary depending on specific circumstances, but in all cases it is important to stay on the schedule as stated by the health care provider giving the vaccine.

How Do I Know If I Have HBV?

Because the symptoms vary so much, the only way to know for sure if you have HBV is to have your blood tested for hepatitis B. The blood test may not, however, indicate the presence of the virus shortly after infection.

Hepatitis B Vaccine

The hepatitis B vaccine is the best protection against HBV. In general, the CDC recommends the hepatitis B vaccination for all infants, older children and adolescents who were not vaccinated previously and for adults at risk for HBV infection.

The vaccine is prepared from yeast cultures, not from human blood or plasma, and therefore there is no risk of contamination with other bloodborne pathogens or of developing hepatitis from the vaccine. Three doses of the vaccine are given by injection on 3 different dates. (In some situations more than 3 doses may be needed.) The most common adverse reaction to vaccination is soreness at the injection site.

The use of the hepatitis B vaccine along with environmental, engineering and work practice controls can prevent most workplace and occupational infections of HBV.

In addition to employees at risk, the CDC also recommends that certain groups of people should get the hepatitis B vaccine including those who:

- Have unprotected sex with a partner who has HBV or who have sex with more than one partner.
- Have anal sex.
- Use intravenous (IV) recreational drugs.
- Are hemophiliacs.
- Frequently travel to or live in countries where HBV is common.
- Live with someone with chronic HBV.

The vaccine prevents hepatitis B in about 95% of people who get all 3 shots. After receiving all 3 shots, you can be tested to make certain you are protected. This is important if you have a compromised immune system or your job frequently exposes you to human blood.

The Standard requires employers to offer the hepatitis B vaccine to employees at risk for exposure at no cost, at a convenient time and place and during their normal work hours. If travel away from the work site is required, the employer is responsible for the travel cost.

As an employee, you have the right to refuse the vaccine. Common reasons for refusing the vaccine are:

- Documentation exists that you have previously received the hepatitis B series.
- Antibody testing shows you are immune.

- You are allergic to any component of the vaccine.
- Medical evaluation shows the vaccination is not adviseable.

If you choose not to be immunized, you will be asked to sign a declination form. You also have the right to change your mind at a later date and receive the vaccination. A sample declination form is in the back of this Participant Guide.

Employers are required to:

- Offer training and the hepatitis B vaccine before employees start a work assignment.
- Explain to employees that vaccination is voluntary.
- Make certain employees receive proper medical treatment following any exposure incident, regardless of their vaccination history, and are offered the vaccination if they have not received it earlier.

Prevention of HBV Infection

The hepatitis B vaccine is the best way to prevent becoming infected with hepatitis B. If you choose not to be vaccinated, however, you can prevent infection by protecting yourself from exposure to blood and OPIM. These include the same protections you should take to avoid all bloodborne pathogens:

- Using barriers to prevent contact with any blood and OPIM
- Handling sharps with extreme care
- Avoiding recreational IV drugs
- Protected sexual contact
- Avoiding the sharing of contaminated needles, syringes or other injection drug equipment
- Avoiding tattooing and body piercing if the tools are not sterile
- Not sharing any personal care items that may be contaminated with blood

The next module discusses these guidelines in more detail.

Learning Checkpoint 2

1. More than one blood test may be necessary in some cases to determine if a person has HBV.   **True**   **False**

2. An employer is required to provide the hepatitis B vaccine at no cost to employees at risk.   **True**   **False**

3. HBV may enter the body through − (Circle all that apply.)

   a. skin abrasions.

   b. open cuts.

   c. mucous membranes in the nose or mouth.

   d. mucous membrances in the eyes.

4. Which of the following are the most likely body fluids to cause HBV infection? (Circle all that apply.)

   a. Semen

   b. Vaginal secretions

   c. Blood

   d. Sweat

5. After about 2 years, a person who carries HBV is no longer infectious to others.   **True**   **False**

Hepatitis C

Hepatitis C is a liver disease caused by the **hepatitis C virus (HCV).** This virus lives in the blood of people with the disease and is spread via the blood. The time from exposure to developing HCV averages 45 days with a range of 14-180 days. The CDC reports an estimated 2.4 million people in the United States have chronic HCV infection and about 50,000 new infections occur each year. HCV does not always cause serious health problems. Many people who carry HCV have some liver damage but do not feel sick from it. In others, cirrhosis of the liver may develop, resulting in eventual liver failure. The CDC estimates over 15,000 people in the United States die from HCV-related illness per year.[3]

How Is HCV Spread?

In the general population, HCV spreads most often through sharing of contaminated needles, syringes or other injection drug equipment. HCV infection may also result from unclean tattoo or body piercing tools, improper disposal of body piercing tools or from sharing toothbrushes, razors or any other item contaminated with blood. HCV can also be transmitted from a pregnant woman to the fetus and, more rarely, through sexual contact.

For those employed in health care facilities, the primary risk of HCV transmission is by direct contact with infectious blood through an accidental needlestick or injury with other sharps.

[3](https://www.cdc.gov/hepatitis/hcv/hcvfaq.htm#section1 Accessed 09/20/21)

Symptoms of HCV

Most people with hepatitis C do not have symptoms. However, some people may feel one or more of the following symptoms:

- Fever
- Fatigue
- Dark urine
- Clay-colored stool
- Abdominal pain
- Loss of appetite
- Nausea
- Vomiting
- Joint pain
- Jaundice (**Figure 2-6**)

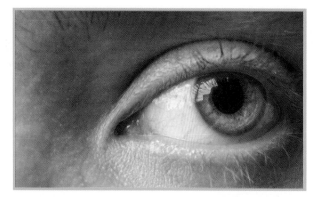

Figure 2-6 *Yellowish color of the whites of eyes may be a sign of jaundice.*

How Do I Know If I Have HCV?

Several different blood tests can be done to determine if you have HCV. A false positive test (a test result appears positive when the person is not infected) can occur with HCV tests, however. Therefore, anyone who tests positive should have a follow-up test. False negative test results may also occur with HCV. These usually occur with testing done shortly after infection when antibodies have not yet developed and therefore cannot be accurately measured. A different type of blood test may then be recommended.

The CDC recommends HCV testing for the following groups of people:

- Health care workers who have been exposed to HCV-positive blood
- Anyone who has used recreational IV drugs
- Anyone who received a blood transfusion or organ transplant or was on kidney dialysis prior to 1992
- Anyone treated with a blood product prior to 1987
- Anyone with signs of liver disease

Testing is important for these people because, if necessary, treatment can be given to protect the liver from additional damage, and people who know they are HCV carriers can take preventive measures to avoid spreading HCV to others.

Prevention of HCV Infection

There currently is no vaccine available for HCV. Therefore, preventive measures are very important. The following are recommended preventive practices:

- Handle needles and other sharps with caution, and follow barrier practices to prevent contact with blood and OPIM (**Module 3**).
- Avoid recreational IV drug use, and never reuse or share syringes or drug paraphernalia.
- Do not share toothbrushes, razors or other personal care items that may be contaminated with blood (**Figure 2-7**).
- Remember the health risks associated with tattoos and body piercing if tools are not sterile or sanitary practices are not followed.

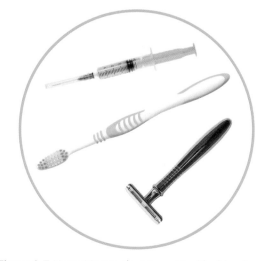

Figure 2-7 *Hepatitis may be transmitted by blood on any personal item.*

Learning Checkpoint 3

1. HCV can be spread through any exposure to saliva, sweat or semen.　　　　**True　　　False**
2. The vaccine that prevents HBV is also effective for HCV.　　　　**True　　　False**
3. Circle symptoms which may be present with HCV:

   a. Nausea　　　　　　　　　　　　**d.** Loss of appetite

   b. Hair loss　　　　　　　　　　　**e.** Sores that do not heal

   c. Abdominal pain　　　　　　　　**f.** Fatigue

4. HCV can cause eventual liver failure.　　　　**True　　　False**

Human Immunodeficiency Virus and Acquired Immunodeficiency Syndrome

Human immunodeficiency virus (HIV) is the virus that can lead to **acquired immunodeficiency syndrome (AIDS).** There are 2 types of HIV: HIV-1 and HIV-2. In the United States, the term HIV primarily refers to HIV-1 because HIV-2 is largely confined to western Africa. Both types of HIV destroy specific blood cells, called CD4+T cells, which are crucial to helping the body fight diseases. AIDS is the late stage of HIV infection, when a person's immune system is severely damaged and has difficulty fighting diseases and certain cancers. Prior to the development of certain medications, people with HIV could progress to AIDS in just a few years. But now, people can live much longer, even decades, before they develop AIDS.

How Is HIV Spread?

HIV is transmitted through an infected person's body fluids. This includes:

- Blood
- Semen
- Vaginal secretions
- Breast milk
- Other body fluids or OPIM if blood is present

Although HIV can sometimes be detected in saliva, tears, urine, cerebrospinal fluid and amniotic fluid, exposure to these fluids from an infected person does not result in transmission of the virus. The greatest risk for health care workers involves exposure to the more than 1 million HIV-positive people in the United States, 21% of whom are unaware of their infection.

There are more than 1.1 million HIV-positive people in the United States, 13% of whom are unaware of their infection. Health care workers often come in contact with these carriers when they seek medical care for other health issues.[4]

Some health care workers have been infected with HIV through work-related exposures involving blood or other infected substances (**Figure 2-8**). Infection is most likely to occur with exposure to HIV-contaminated blood, blood components or blood products through:

- Injection through the skin
- Unprotected mucous membranes
- An open skin wound

[4](https://www.cdc.gov/hiv/basics/statistics.html)

Figure 2-8 *In occupational exposures HIV can enter the body in 3 main ways: through mucous membranes such as in the mouth or eyes, by unintentional injection into the body or by entry through any cut or non-intact area of skin.*

Casual contact with those infected with HIV does not result in transmission of the virus. Casual contact includes such things as the following:

• Sharing food, utensils or a drinking glass
• Kissing, hugging or touching
• Being around someone who sneezes or coughs
• Sharing a phone or bathroom

HIV is not an airborne virus, nor can it be contracted from the bite of a mosquito, flea, tick or other bloodsucking vermin.

Symptoms of HIV

Within a few weeks of being infected with HIV, some people develop flu-like symptoms that last for a week or two. Many people with HIV have no symptoms and do not even know they have been infected. People living with HIV may appear and feel healthy for several years, but HIV is still affecting their bodies.

Late-stage HIV (AIDS) symptoms may include the following:

Late-stage HIV (AIDS) symptoms	
• Fatigue	• Swollen lymph nodes
• Poor appetite	• Diarrhea
• Rapid weight loss	• Tiredness
• Fever	• Night sweats
• Skin rashes	• An inability to fight off infection

How Do I Know If I Have HIV?

The only reliable way to determine if a person has HIV is through a blood test. The most commonly used HIV tests detect HIV antibodies, the substances the body creates in response to becoming infected with HIV. Most people will develop detectable antibodies within 2-8 weeks of their infection. 97% of persons will develop detectable antibodies in the first 3 months. Therefore, a person should consider a follow-up test more than 3 months after their last potential exposure to HIV. In extremely rare cases, it can take up to 6 months to develop antibodies to HIV.

Rapid HIV tests also are available that can give results in as little as 20 minutes. A positive HIV test result means a person may be infected with HIV. All positive HIV test results from either rapid or conventional testing must be verified by a second, confirmation HIV test.

Prevention of HIV Infection

No vaccine is currently available for HIV. Therefore, preventive measures are very important. Safe work practice controls significantly reduce the risk of contracting HIV in the workplace or transmitting infectious diseases to victims. These guidelines include the following:

• Regular hand washing
• Use of barriers
• Universal precautions

Module 3 discusses these guidelines in detail. Compared with HBV, HIV does not live long outside the human body and is easily killed with disinfectants.

✎ Learning Checkpoint 4

1. All people develop HIV symptoms 3 months after exposure.	True	False
2. About 13% of all HIV-positive people do not know they have the infection.	True	False
3. HIV can enter the body only through broken skin.	True	False
4. HIV can be contracted by sharing a fork with an infectious person.	True	False

5. What are the most common symptoms of late-stage HIV (AIDS)? (Circle all that apply.)

a. Frequent sneezing	e. Swollen lymph nodes
b. Rapid weight loss	f. Red spots under fingernails
c. Heart attack	g. Skin rashes
d. Fever	h. Fatigue

6. HIV infection can be prevented in health care settings.	True	False

Select Other Diseases Caused by Bloodborne Pathogens

Disease	Pathogen	Mode of Transmission	Common Signs and Symptoms	Prevention	Treatment
Hepatitis A Short-term (not chronic) infection becoming less common with widely used vaccine in the United States	Hepatitis A virus (HAV)	Primarily by fecal-oral route, usually fecally contaminated food or water Anal sex Exposure to blood or OPIM (rare)	Jaundice, fatigue, abdominal pain, loss of appetite, nausea, diarrhea, fever A very small percentage of patients have more serious complications.	Hand washing and good hygiene Vaccination Short-term protection from immune globulin after exposure	No specific treatment 99% of patients fully recover
Hepatitis E Usually occurs in outbreaks in areas with inadequate environmental sanitation; most cases in U.S. result from travel elsewhere. Does not cause chronic liver disease.	Hepatitis E virus (HEV)	Primarily by fecal-oral route, usually fecally contaminated drinking water Person-to-person transmission (rare)	Abdominal pain, loss of appetite, dark urine, fever, jaundice, malaise, nausea and vomiting	Use of clean water supply; avoiding uncooked shellfish, fruits and vegetables No vaccine available	No specific treatment Almost all patients fully recover
Syphilis A bacterial sexually transmitted disease that can cause serious health problems.	Treponema pallidum bacterium	Vaginal, anal or oral sex Mother to fetus	Primary stage: Sore (chancre) on external genitals, vagina, anus or rectum or lips and mouth Secondary stage: Rashes, fever, swollen lymph glands, sore throat, aches, fatigue Late Stage: Internal damage causing uncoordinated movement, paralysis, blindness, dementia	Abstinence from sexual contact Correct and consistent use of latex condoms reduces the risk of transmission	Easily cured with antibiotics in early stages Treatment in late stages less effective

Disease	Pathogen	Mode of Transmission	Common Signs and Symptoms	Prevention	Treatment
Ebola Hemorrhagic Fever Has occurred since 1976 in sporadic outbreaks in Africa. Has not appeared in the United States.	Ebola virus	First transmission at the start of an outbreak is unknown (may be contact with infected animal) Transmitted among humans by contact with infected person's blood or OPIM	Fever, headache, joint and muscle aches, sore throat, weakness; followed by diarrhea, vomiting, stomach pain. Some infected people may have rash, red eyes and internal and external bleeding.	During an outbreak: isolation of Ebola patients and use of barrier devices and all bloodborne pathogen infection control guidelines	Supportive care only; no cure. Still unknown why some patients recover while others die.
Malaria Common in over 100 countries; nearly half of the world population is at risk. 300-500 million cases occur yearly (World Health Organization). A few cases occur annually in the United States	4 different Plasmodium species (parasites)	The bite of a malaria-infected mosquito Blood transfusions Mother to fetus	Fever, flu-like symptoms (shaking chills, headache, muscle aches, fatigue, nausea and vomiting, diarrhea, anemia, jaundice) One type may cause kidney failure, seizures, coma, death	Vaccination and anti-malarial drugs Prevention of mosquito bites	Generally can be cured with prescription drugs, type and length of treatment depending on type of malaria and other factors
West Nile Virus Seasonal epidemic in North America	West Nile virus	Usually by bite of infected mosquito Blood transfusions (rare) Mother to fetus or to infant through breast milk (rare)	No symptoms in 80% of infected people Mild symptoms in 20%: fever, headache, body aches, nausea and vomiting, swollen lymph glands, rash Serious symptoms in 1 in 150 people: high fever, neck stiffness, stupor, coma, tremors, convulsions, vision loss, paralysis	Prevention of mosquito bites Elimination of mosquito breeding sites	No specific treatment Supportive care for severe cases

3

Preventing Infection from Bloodborne Pathogens

Module Objectives

By the end of this module, you will be able to:

- List the 4 types of strategies to reduce occupational exposure to bloodborne pathogens required by the OSHA Standard.
- Describe the general guidelines for the use of these engineering controls: sharps containers, hand washing facilities and eye wash stations and warning labels.
- Describe the general guidelines for these work practice controls: hand washing, decontamination and sterilization, handling sharps, regulated waste handling and disposal, laundry and work area restrictions.

- Describe the general guidelines for the use of these items of personal protective equipment: gloves, jumpsuits, aprons, lab coats, goggles and eye shields, face shields and face masks, caps and booties.
- Define the principle of universal precautions.
- Describe what actions to take if you are exposed to blood or OPIM.
- Describe what your employer is required to do if you are exposed.
- List what information must be in your employer's Exposure Control Plan.

Video Review

1. What are the four strategies OSHA standards require to reduce occupational exposure to bloodborne pathogens?

_____

_____

_____

_____

The OSHA Occupational Exposure to Bloodborne Pathogens Standard (the Standard) requires employers to use 4 types of strategies to reduce occupational exposure to bloodborne pathogens:

1. Engineering controls
2. Work practice controls
3. Personal protective equipment
4. Universal precautions

In addition, the Standard requires having procedures in place in the event an exposure does occur and maintaining an Exposure Control Plan.

Engineering Controls

OSHA defines **engineering controls** as devices that isolate or remove the bloodborne pathogen hazard from the workplace. Many kinds of devices have been developed to increase safety in the workplace. These devices include needleless IV systems, self-sheathing needles or syringes, eye wash stations, hand washing facilities, sharps containers and biohazard labels. These all have an important role in reducing the risk of exposure to bloodborne pathogens.

Sharps

Sharp is a general term for any device or item that may accidentally penetrate the skin of a person handling it. Examples of sharps are needles, scissors, scalpels, disposable razors used for shaving in nursing homes, health care and correctional facilities, and broken glassware (**Figure 3-1**).

Hollow bore needles pose one of the greatest risks to health care workers. Safer needleless systems are now used in many settings for administering medications. Other systems have needle shields, retractable needles or other protective devices. Employers are not necessarily required to use the latest devices but must evaluate the feasibility of such devices annually (**Figure 3-2**). Employers must document which

commercially available engineering controls are being considered and whether they will be implemented. OSHA requires employers to include input from non-managerial employees in the selection process.

Approved sharps containers must be available in appropriate places for safe disposal of used sharps. These containers must be leak proof, resistant to puncture and other damage, able to be securely closed, upright and labeled with a biohazard warning (**Figure 3-3**). Sharps containers must be replaced routinely so they do not overfill. The containers for reusable sharps such as scissors are not required to be closable, as these containers likely will be reused.

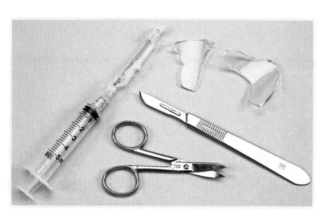

Figure 3-1 *Different types of sharps.*

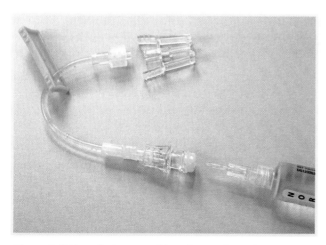

Figure 3-2 *New devices provide safeguards against an unintentional needlestick.*

Figure 3-3 *Wall-mounted and cart-mounted sharps containers.*

Hand Washing Facilities and Eye Wash Stations

When possible, hand washing facilities must be provided for all employees. When not possible, alcohol-based hand rubs may be provided instead. Eye wash stations should be available when appropriate for flushing contaminants from the eyes (**Figure 3-4**).

Figure 3-4 *An eye wash station is used to flush a substance that has splashed in the eyes.*

Warning Labels

Warning labels are required to be prominently displayed on the following:

- Containers for waste that may contain contaminated materials (biohazardous waste)
- Freezers and refrigerators used for blood or other potentially infectious materials (OPIM)

- Containers used to transport, ship or store blood or OPIM
- Contaminated equipment until proper cleaning procedures are complete
- Laundry bags used to hold and transport contaminated clothing
- Entrances to places containing potentially infectious materials

All potentially infectious waste must be disposed of in properly labeled red containers or in containers clearly marked with a red, orange or orange-red label with the universal biohazard symbol (**Figure 3-5**).

Figure 3-5 *The universal biohazard symbol.*

 ANTISEPTIC HAND CLEANSER

If antiseptic towelettes or antibacterial hand washing liquid is used without water for the initial cleaning after an exposure, a thorough scrubbing with soap and water is still needed as soon as possible.

Learning Checkpoint 1

1. Sharps include scissors, disposable razors used for shaving in nursing homes and needles.

   True   False

2. Engineering controls include: (Circle all that apply.)
   a. Needleless injection systems
   b. Eye wash stations
   c. Biohazard labels

3. Employers are required to purchase all newly developed devices that help prevent employees from exposure to bloodborne pathogens.

   True   False

4. Name at least 3 places biohazardous warning labels must appear:

   _____

   _____

   _____

Work Practice Controls

Work practice controls are controls that reduce the likelihood of exposure by altering the manner in which a task is performed. Depending upon the environment, work practice controls might include using personal protective equipment (PPE), hand washing, decontaminating and sterilizing equipment and areas, safely handling sharps, correctly disposing of wastes, safely handling laundry and good personal habits (Figure 3-6).

Hand Hygiene

Hand hygiene means performing hand washing or using antiseptic hand wash or alcohol-based hand rubs. Hand hygiene is important because bacteria can survive for days on equipment and other surfaces (e.g., bed rails, IV pumps, computer keyboards). It is a simple but very important step for preventing the transmission of bloodborne pathogens.

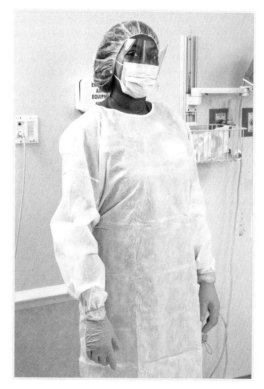

Figure 3-6 *Safe work practice controls include use of personal protective equipment.*

Hand Washing

The following are general guidelines to use with hand washing:

- Wash any exposed skin, ideally with antibacterial soap, as soon after an exposure as possible.
- While washing, be gentle with any scabs or sores.
- Wash all surfaces, including the backs of hands, wrists, between the fingers and under fingernails.
- Wash hands immediately after removing gloves or other PPE.

Antiseptic towelettes and waterless antibacterial hand washing liquid can be used when soap and running water are not available. If one of these methods is used for the initial cleaning after a potential exposure, however, a thorough scrubbing with soap and water is still recommended as soon as possible and is required if there was exposure to blood or OPIM.

Alcohol-Based Hand Rubs

Use of alcohol-based hand rubs is the preferred method of hand hygiene in health care settings in all situations except when hands are visibly dirty or contaminated. Hand rubs are encouraged in health care settings because they require less time to use and are more accessible than sinks. Other benefits of hand rubs include their ability to reduce bacterial counts on hands more than soap and water alone and are less drying and irritating to the skin than soap and water (**Figure 3-7**).

HAND WASHING

Before handling any potentially infectious materials, know where the nearest hand washing facility is. You can use facilities such as restrooms, janitor closets and laboratory sinks, as long as soap is available. Do not use sinks in areas where food is prepared. Merely wetting the hands will not prevent infection.

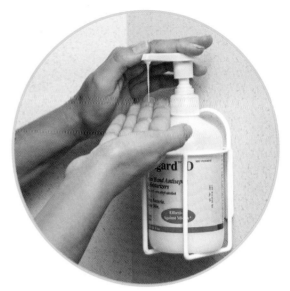

Figure 3-7 *Alcohol-based hand rubs reduce bacterial counts on hands.*

Decontamination and Sterilization

OSHA defines **decontamination** as the use of physical or chemical means to remove, inactivate or destroy bloodborne pathogens on a surface or item so it is no longer infectious. To **sterilize** something means to use a chemical or physical procedure to destroy all microbial life on the item. Use the following general guidelines for decontamination and sterilization:

- All reusable sharps, such as knives, scissors and scalpels, must be cleaned and sterilized after being used:
  - Before cleaning, store sharps in a container with a wide opening.
  - Use forceps or tongs to remove contaminated sharps from containers.
- Decontaminate equipment and working surfaces, bench tops and floors with an approved commercial disinfectant or a 10% bleach solution:
  - At the end of a work shift
  - As surfaces become obviously contaminated
  - After any spill of blood or OPIM
- Disinfect personal items, such as jewelry and nail brushes, after hand washing.
- Use utensils, such as tongs or a dustpan, to clean up broken glass and other contaminated materials for disposal in a sharps container.

Hand Washing

1. Wet hands with water.

2. Apply enough soap to cover all hand surfaces.

3. Rub hands palm to palm.

4. Rub right palm over left, with interlaced fingers and vice versa.

5. Rub palm to palm with fingers interlaced.

6. Rub backs of fingers to opposing palms with fingers interlocked.

7. Rub left thumb clasped in right palm and vise versa.

8. Rotational rubbing, backwards and forwards with clasped fingers of right hand in left palm and vice versa.

9. Rinse hands with water.

10. Dry hands thoroughly with paper towel and dispose of properly.

11. Use towel to turn off faucet and open door.

This procedure should take 40-60 seconds.

Complete Skill

Cleaning Broken Sharps and a Contaminated Spill

Learn the Skill

☐ 1. Wear heavy utility gloves and other personal protective equipment to protect yourself while cleaning the spill.

☐ 2. Bring supplies and hazardous waste containers to the location of the spill.

☐ 3. Use tongs or other means to pick up any broken glass, and dispose of it in an appropriate sharps container.

☐ 4. Absorb the entire spill with paper towels and dispose of them in the biohazard container before using disinfectant.

☐ 5. Disinfect the area thoroughly with an approved disinfectant.

☐ 6. Remove your gloves and wash your hands.

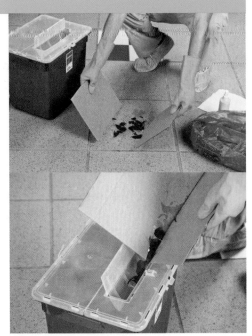

Step 3

Step 4

🔔 ## PICKING UP SHARPS OR BROKEN GLASS

The Standard states that employees should never pick up broken glass or other sharps with gloved or bare hands. Always use tongs or some other device to pick them up. Do not use a vacuum cleaner. Never touch broken glass with your hands. Have all supplies ready before starting cleanup.

Step 6

☐ **Complete Skill**

Using a Commercial Body Fluid Disposal Kit

Learn the Skill

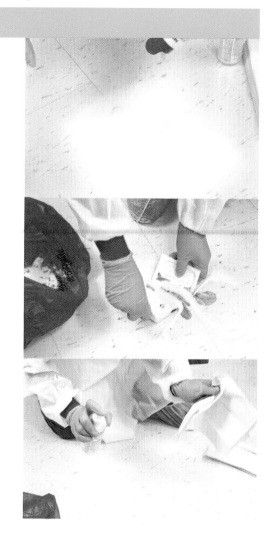

☐ 1. Wearing disposable apron, eye shield/ face mask, shoe covers and medical exam gloves, sprinkle absorbent over the blood spill until fluid is absorbed completely.

☐ 2. Use a scoop and scraper to scrape up the absorbent material. Discard the material scoop and scraper in red biohazard bag.

☐ 3. Spray disinfectant/cleaner over the spill area. Allow it to remain wet for about 10 minutes. Use paper towels to wipe up the disinfectant. Discard paper towels in red biohazard bag.

☐ 4. Discard apron, eye shield/face mask, shoe covers and medical exam gloves in red biohazard bag and dispose of the bag according to federal, state and local regulations. Wash hands thoroughly with soap and water.

☐ **Complete Skill**

Figure 3-8 *Sharps container inside an ambulance.*

Handling Sharps

Guidelines for safe handling of sharps include the following:

- Employers must put sharps disposal containers in easily accessible areas where sharps are used (**Figure 3-8**).
- Needles must not be recapped, removed, bent, sheared or broken.
- The entire needle/syringe assembly must be disposed of in a sharps container.
- Only when medically necessary, a mechanical device may be used to recap a contaminated needle or remove it from a disposable syringe. OSHA requires that the exposure control plan must specify when, why and how this is done and by whom.

Regulated Waste Handling and Disposal

The Standard has provisions to protect employees during the containment, storage and transport of regulated waste other than contaminated sharps. However, OSHA does not regulate the final disposal of regulated waste. According to OSHA, the final disposal of regulated waste must be in accordance with applicable regulations of the United States, states and territories, and political subdivisions of states and territories.

Regulated waste includes:

- Blood or OPIM in liquid or semi-liquid state
- Items contaminated with blood or OPIM that could release liquid or semi-liquid blood or OPIM if squeezed
- Items with dried blood that could be spread by handling
- Contaminated sharps
- Lab specimens containing blood or OPIM

All containers intended for disposal of potentially infectious materials should be clearly marked with the universal biohazard symbol (**Figure 3-5**). The facility must follow approved procedures for disposing of regulated waste and disinfecting equipment for reuse.

Laundry

Uniforms, clothing and cloth supplies should be kept free from contamination when possible. Clothing intended to prevent contact with blood that becomes contaminated with blood or OPIM must be put in special laundry bags that are clearly labeled and color-coded to be sent to an approved laundry facility for cleaning. OSHA has stated that, "home laundering is unacceptable because the employer cannot ensure that proper handling or laundering procedures are being followed and because contamination could migrate to the homes of employees."[1]

Employers are responsible for cleaning, laundering and/or disposing of personal protective equipment.

Many agencies use yellow bags with the biohazard symbol affixed to them to avoid confusion with red bags, which usually contain materials for disposal (**Figure 3-9**). Anyone handling contaminated laundry must be trained to handle bloodborne pathogens and must wear appropriate PPE.

[1]*(CPL 02-02-069 XIII.D.16 Accessed 9/22/21)*

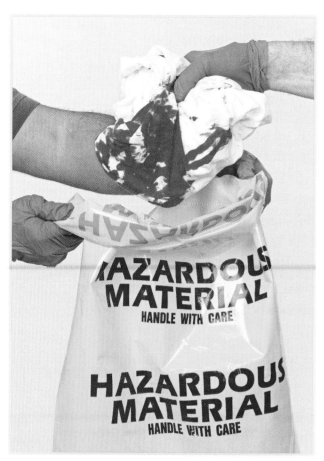

Figure 3-9 *Biohazard laundry bag for contaminated clothing.*

Work Area Restrictions

When working in an area where bloodborne pathogen exposure may occur, prevent entry of pathogens into your mouth or eyes by keeping your hands away from your face. In general, follow these guidelines:

• Do not smoke.
• Do not put on lip balm, hand lotion or cosmetics.
• Do not eat or drink.
• Do not handle your contact lenses.
• Do not store food or beverages in places where blood is stored or handled, including in refrigerators, freezers, shelves or cabinets or on countertops or bench tops where blood or OPIM are present.
• Do not put pencils, pens or other objects in your mouth where potentially infectious materials may be present.
• Do not use a sink that is used for food preparation for any other cleanup.

Notes:

CONTAMINATED CLOTHING

Never take contaminated clothing home to wash. Keep extra clothing at work in case your street clothes become contaminated and must be sent to the approved laundry facility.

✎ Learning Checkpoint 2

1. If you wash your hands with waterless soap, further cleansing is not necessary.   **True**   **False**

2. Equipment must be decontaminated with a 25% bleach solution.   **True**   **False**

3. Regulated waste includes: (Circle all that apply.)

   a. Contaminated sharps   c. Lab specimens containing OPIM

   b. Clothing with dried blood on it   d. Dressings and bandages that could release blood if squeezed

4. Eating in an area used for lab research on human tissue specimens poses little risk and is generally acceptable as long as you wear gloves.   **True**   **False**

5. When should you always clean under your fingernails when washing your hands?

   _____

6. Never use a vacuum cleaner to clean a floor of potentially infectious material.   **True**   **False**

7. Describe what to do if your clothing briefly contacts a spill that may contain an infectious liquid.

   _____

Personal Protective Equipment

Personal protective equipment consists of barriers such as gloves, jumpsuits or aprons, eye shields or goggles, face masks or face shields and caps and booties you wear to protect yourself from exposure to blood and OPIM. The Standard requires your employer to provide you with appropriate PPE at no cost to you. Your employer also must train you in how to use this equipment and must clean, repair or replace it as needed.

In any situation where exposure to bloodborne pathogens is a possibility, wear your PPE.

Figure 3-10 *Wear gloves whenever you may contact blood or OPIM.*

Gloves

Gloves are a type of barrier which, like other barriers, separate you from potentially infectious materials (**Figure 3-10**). Medical exam gloves suitable for protection from bloodborne pathogens are made of nitrile, vinyl, latex or other waterproof materials. For added barrier protection, 2 pairs of gloves may be worn together in some situations. At a minimum, gloves must be used where there is reasonable anticipation of employee hand contact with blood or OPIM and when handling or touching contaminated surfaces or items. Here, the term "contaminated" means the presence or reasonable anticipated presence of blood or OPIM, rather than just being "visibly" contaminated.

Putting on Gloves

Learn the Skill

☐ **1.** Pull glove onto 1 hand.

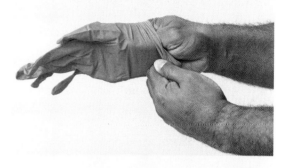

☐ **2.** Pull glove tight.

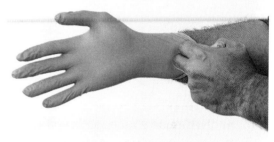

☐ **3.** Put on other glove.

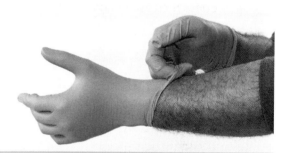

☐ **Complete Skill**

When using gloves, you must remember to:

- **Check that your gloves are intact.** If a hole or tear is present, replace the glove immediately with a new one.
- **Not use petroleum-based hand lotions.** These lotions may cause latex gloves to disintegrate.
- **Remove contaminated gloves carefully.** Do not touch any part of the contaminated material on the outside of the gloves.
- **Dispose of gloves properly.** After working with any material that may be infected by bloodborne pathogens, dispose of your gloves in a container clearly marked for biohazardous waste.

LATEX ALLERGY

People who frequently wear latex gloves have a potential risk of developing a latex allergy. This reaction may include a skin rash or even cause difficulty breathing. If you experience signs of an allergy when wearing gloves, ask your employer for latex-free or hypoallergenic gloves made of nitrile or vinyl.

Removing Contaminated Gloves

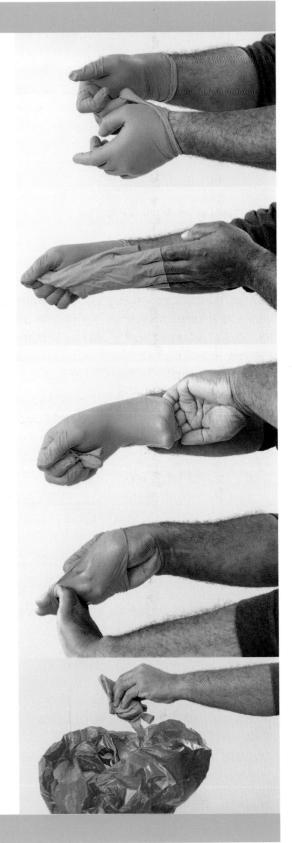

☐   **1.** With your gloved dominant hand, grasp the other glove at the wrist or palm and pull it away from the hand.

☐   **2.** Pull the glove the rest of the way off.

☐   **3.** Holding the removed glove balled up in the palm of your gloved hand, insert fingers of your non-dominant hand under the cuff of the remaining glove.

☐   **4.** Remove the glove by stretching it up and away from the hand turning it inside out as you pull it off.

☐   **5.** Dispose of gloves in a biohazard container, and wash your hands.

☐   **Complete Skill**

Protective Body Clothing

Jumpsuits, aprons, lab coats and gowns are sometimes worn to protect clothing from contamination by blood and OPIM. These barriers are available in different thicknesses and materials. Any articles of clothing that become contaminated with blood should be removed immediately and handled as carefully as any contaminated item. Avoid contact with your skin, and put the article in a clearly marked biohazardous laundry bag.

Goggles and Eye Shlelds

Certain occupations or work conditions involve a risk of being splashed in the face by blood or substances contaminated with bloodborne pathogens. Because the eyes are surrounded by mucous membranes, a splash in the eyes may allow bloodborne pathogens into the body. Use of barrier devices is therefore often essential. Eye protection is also recommended when cleaning spills or performing first aid.

PPE for the eyes includes goggles and safety glasses with side shields. Face shields also protect the eyes (**Figure 3-11**). If you are wearing prescription eyeglasses, you must use side shields. Both the glasses and the side shields must be decontaminated according to the schedule set by your employer.

Figure 3-11 *Different kinds of eye protection are available.*

Figure 3-12 *Different kinds of face protection are available.*

Figure 3-13 *Pocket face masks and face shields are used during CPR.*

Face Shields and Face Masks

Face shields protect the eyes, mouth and nose from splashes and contaminants. Face masks protect the mouth and nose. When worn with goggles or safety glasses, face masks help protect the whole face (**Figure 3-12**). Pocket face masks and face shields are used when giving rescue breaths during cardiopulmonary resuscitation (CPR). Both types of devices offer protection from the victim's saliva and other fluids, as well as from the victim's exhaled air when equipped with a 1-way valve (**Figure 3-13**).

Caps and Booties

The forehead and the hair may be covered by a waterproof disposable cap, and shoes or boots by waterproof, disposable booties. Both provide additional barriers to bloodborne pathogens.

Improvising Personal Protective Equipment

In unexpected or extreme circumstances, you may not have PPE with you when potentially exposed to bloodborne pathogens. Be creative in using items at hand to avoid contact with potentially infectious material. Using a plastic bag, a sheet or a towel or even removing an article of clothing to use as a barrier is better than being unprotected **(Figure 3-14)**. Dispose of or decontaminate any articles you use as barriers as you would any contaminated item.

Disposing of Contaminated Personal Protective Equipment

Different forms of protective equipment require different disposal methods. Your employer may request that you put articles such as used gloves in a designated container for storage until they are disposed of. Contaminated clothing may be stored in clearly labeled bags until it is decontaminated, laundered or properly disposed of.

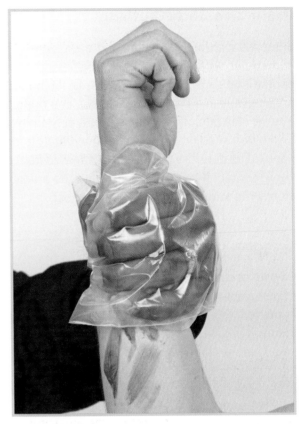

Figure 3-14 *Always use a barrier – improvise when necessary.*

Learning Checkpoint 3

1. Mucous membranes of the face can be protected by wearing a mask and goggles. **True**   **False**

2. Circle items below considered personal protective equipment:

   a. Latex gloves
   b. Face shield
   c. Face mask
   d. Booties
   e. Jumpsuit
   f. Goggles

3. It is acceptable to patch a small hole in your gloves with a Band-Aid. **True**   **False**

4. Used gloves should be disposed of like hazardous waste. **True**   **False**

5. Your employer should arrange for you to purchase your necessary personal protective equipment at an employee discount. **True**   **False**

Universal Precautions

Universal precautions is a phrase describing safety guidelines in which all blood and OPIM are handled as if they are contaminated. When universal precautions are followed, it does not matter whether you know the source of the substance. Under universal precautions, you treat all materials as if they are infected with bloodborne pathogens. This includes the following:

- Blood
- Semen
- Vaginal secretions
- Saliva that may contain blood
- Cerebrospinal fluid
- Synovial fluid
- Pleural fluid
- Any body fluid where blood is visible
- Any body fluid that cannot be identified

Following universal precautions means using PPE and following all the safe work practice controls described in this guide.

Body Substance Isolation

Body substance isolation (BSI) is an alternative approach to universal precautions. BSI guidelines define all body fluids and substances as infectious. Since OSHA now requires all body fluids to be managed with universal precautions, this approach is essentially the same as BSI.

Standard Precautions

The health care industry uses the term standard precautions to describe the guidelines for handling blood and OPIM. According to the CDC, standard precautions combine the major features of universal precautions and body substance isolation and are based on the principle that all blood, body fluids, secretions, excretions except sweat, non-in-contact skin and mucous membranes may contain transmissible infectious agents.[2]

Standard precautions include a group of infection prevention practices that apply to all patients, regardless of suspected or confirmed infection status, in any setting in which health care is delivered. They include hand hygiene, use of gloves, gown, mask, eye protection or face shield, depending on the anticipated exposure, and safe injection practices. Standard precautions are considered more stringent than universal precautions alone.

Emergency Procedures for an Unexpected Exposure Incident

Even when you follow all safety guidelines and universal precautions, an unexpected exposure can occur. If so, both you and your employer need to take immediate action. Employers are required to inform you how to make an incident report in case you are exposed. A sample exposure incident report form can be found on pages 50-51.

If you are exposed take the following actions:

- If blood or OPIM splashes in your eyes or other mucous membranes, flush the area with running water for 20 minutes if possible.
- Wash any exposed area well with soap, using an antibacterial soap if possible.
- Treat any scabs and sores gently when cleaning your skin.
- Report the exposure to your supervisor as soon as possible on the day the exposure occurs to assure prompt evaluation.
- Save any potentially contaminated object for testing purposes.
- Seek medical care as soon as possible.

After receiving your report, your employer must do the following:

- Identify and document the person or other source of the blood or OPIM.

[2](The Centers for Disease Control and Prevention, Guideline for Isolation Precautions: "Preventing Transmission of Infectious Agents in Healthcare Settings 2007," p. 66)

Universal Precautions and All Body Fluids

Previously, universal precautions did not apply to other body fluids, such as nasal secretions, sweat, tears and urine and feces, which were not considered potentially infectious.

Currently, however, an OSHA written interpretation states universal precautions should apply to all body fluids because it is impossible to know by looking whether these other body fluids may contain traces of blood. Therefore, assume all body fluids may be infectious and always follow universal precautions.

Required Information when Reporting Exposure Incidents

- Date and time of your exposure
- Your job title/classification
- Your work location where the exposure happened
- Activity you were performing at the time of the exposure
- Your training for that activity
- Engineering controls (devices and equipment) you were using at the time of the exposure
- Preventive work practice controls you were using at the time of the exposure
- Personal protective equipment you were using at the time of the exposure

- Obtain consent to test the source person's blood and arrange for testing the person (unless he or she is already known to be infectious). If the source refuses testing or if the source is unknown, the employee is still offered evaluation.
- Inform you of the test results.
- Arrange for you to have your blood tested if you consent.
- Arrange for you to receive counseling and medical care as needed.

The treatment and follow-up medical care depends on the type of exposure: the substance involved, the route of transmission and the severity of the exposure. Treatment may include a hepatitis B vaccination or treatment with hepatitis B immune globulin.

An **exposure incident report form** is kept in the employee's confidential file (**Figure 3-15**). By federal law, employers must maintain strict confidentiality about any exposure incident.

Figure 3-15 *After an exposure your employer will work with you to arrange any needed testing and treatment.*

Exposure Incident

Don't delay acting if you are exposed to blood or OPIM. Every minute counts in preventing pathogens from entering the body.

Exposure Control Plans

OSHA requires employers to have an **Exposure Control Plan** to prevent exposure to bloodborne pathogens. Your employer's Exposure Control Plan should do the following:

- Identify the job positions and individuals to receive training.
- Establish necessary engineering controls and work practice controls.
- Specify PPE to be used.
- Require using universal precautions.
- State the opportunity for a hepatitis B vaccination.
- Include other measures appropriate for your specific work environment.

The Exposure Control Plan must be reviewed and updated at least annually and whenever necessary to reflect any changes in work practice controls related to possible exposure to bloodborne pathogens. The plan should also describe how improved safety devices are to be evaluated for possible use. It is essential that employees who are covered under the Exposure Control Plan be trained according to the plan. These employees also must have access to the plan.

The Standard requires that employers inform new employees about their plan and conduct training before performing any work tasks that would put you at risk for an exposure. Refresher training is required annually or whenever changes are made to policies and procedures (**Figure 3-16**).

Figure 3-16 *Employees have the right to see the Exposure Control Plan.*

A sample exposure control plan is included in the back of this Participant Guide.

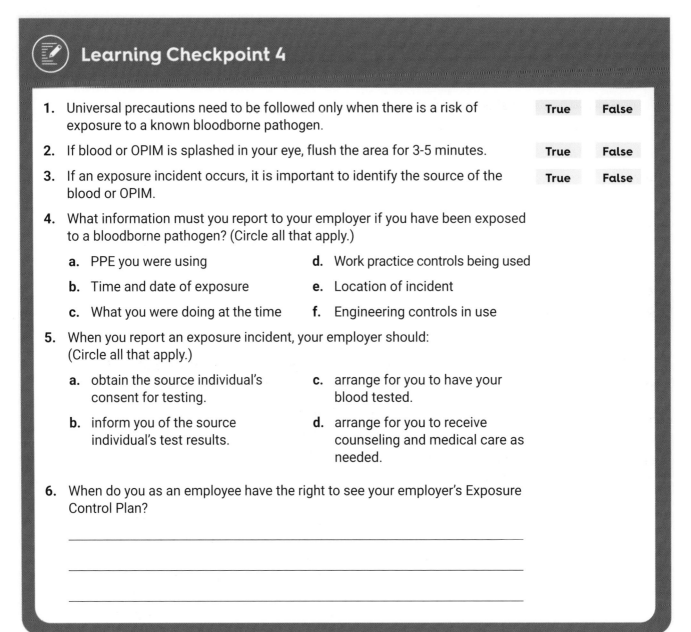

Learning Checkpoint 4

1. Universal precautions need to be followed only when there is a risk of exposure to a known bloodborne pathogen.   True   False

2. If blood or OPIM is splashed in your eye, flush the area for 3-5 minutes.   True   False

3. If an exposure incident occurs, it is important to identify the source of the blood or OPIM.   True   False

4. What information must you report to your employer if you have been exposed to a bloodborne pathogen? (Circle all that apply.)

    a. PPE you were using   d. Work practice controls being used

    b. Time and date of exposure   e. Location of incident

    c. What you were doing at the time f. Engineering controls in use

5. When you report an exposure incident, your employer should: (Circle all that apply.)

    a. obtain the source individual's consent for testing.

    c. arrange for you to have your blood tested.

    b. inform you of the source individual's test results.

    d. arrange for you to receive counseling and medical care as needed.

6. When do you as an employee have the right to see your employer's Exposure Control Plan?

    _____

    _____

    _____

Airborne Pathogens

Module Objectives

By the end of this module, you will be able to:

- List the different types of airborne pathogens.
- List high-risk workplaces for airborne disease.
- Explain the difference between an epidemic and a pandemic.
- Describe the method of infection, symptoms, and special considerations for tuberculosis, influenza, and COVID-19 infections.
- Describe what to do if you are experiencing symptoms of COVID-19.
- Explain administrative, environmental, and respiratory protection controls for preventing disease transmission.
- Describe the types of personal protective equipment (PPE) used to minimize transmission of airborne diseases.

OSHA regulations do not currently specify specific employee protections from airborne pathogens in the same manner as the Occupational Exposure to Bloodborne Pathogens Standard specifies protections against bloodborne pathogens. OSHA does expect employers to protect employees from known hazards, however, which in certain settings can include airborne pathogens such as tuberculosis (TB). OSHA enforces this protection for workers through the Occupational Safety and Health Act of 1970 or the General Duty Clause (Public Law 91-596).

What Are Airborne Pathogens?

Airborne pathogens are disease-causing microorganisms spread from person to person in the form of droplet nuclei in the air. There are three types of airborne pathogens:

- Viral
- Bacterial
- Fungal

Meningitis, influenza, pneumonia, TB and COVID-19 are examples of diseases transmitted through the air. This Module focuses on TB because that is a common airborne disease for which employees may be at risk. Influenza and COVID-19 are also included in the Module because they are common airborne pathogens. Many of the precautions taken to prevent TB will also lower the risk of infection from other airborne pathogens such as influenza.

Airborne pathogens differ from bloodborne pathogens in that they are spread by inhalation of the germ. An infectious person's coughing, sneezing, laughing or singing can send tiny droplets of moisture into the air that contain the pathogen. Depending on the environment, these contaminants can remain airborne for several hours.

Although an airborne pathogen may be transmitted if the pathogen is inhaled, exposure to airborne pathogens does not always result in infection. The likelihood of infection depends on the following:

- How contagious the infectious person is
- Where the exposure occurs
- How long the exposure lasts
- How healthy you are at the time of the exposure

The likelihood of airborne infection depends on how contagious the infectious person is, where the exposure occurs, how long the exposure lasts, and how healthy you are at the time of exposure.

According to the CDC, employees in certain workplaces also face a greater risk of exposure. These workplaces include but are not limited to the following:

- Correctional facilities
- Drug and treatment centers
- Health care facilities (emergency departments, patient rooms, medical offices and clinics, home-based health care, Emergency Medical Services; nursing homes; long-term care facilities)
- Homeless shelters
- Long-term care facilities
- Morgues

Epidemic and Pandemic

Airborne pathogens can lead to epidemics and pandemics.

An Epidemic is an an outbreak of a disease in a community or region that affects a large portion of the population. During an epidemic, the disease is actively spreading and spread is not under control. In an epidemic, a sudden increase in the number of disease cases is seen above what epidemiologists would normally expect.

A Pandemic is an outbreak that spreads throughout the world over several countries or continents. COVID-19 is the most recent pandemic, and it has significantly impacted all parts of the world.

Tuberculosis

Tuberculosis is caused by a specific bacterium, Mycobacterium (**Figure 4-1**) that can lead to infection and disease. People with latent TB infection do not feel sick and do not have any symptoms. The only sign of TB infection is a positive TB test.

People with latent TB infection are not infectious and cannot spread TB infection to others.

In some people, TB bacteria overcome the defenses of the immune system and begin to multiply, resulting in the progression from latent TB infection to TB disease.

TB disease was once the leading cause of death in the United States. Starting in the 1940s, scientists discovered the first of several medicines used to treat TB and, as a result, TB slowly began to decrease in the United States. However, in the 1970s and early 1980s, TB

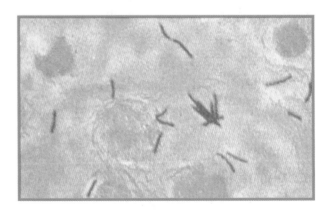

Figure 4-1 *The bacteria that causes tuberculosis.*

control efforts were neglected. As a result, between 1985 and 1992 the number of TB cases increased. With increased attention to the TB problem, the number of persons with TB has been declining steadily since 1992.

In 2019, TB rates decreased to 2.7 cases per 100,000 population. But TB is still a problem; 8,916 cases were reported in 2019 in the United States.[1]

Tuberculosis usually affects the lungs, but it can also affect the brain, spine, lymph nodes or kidneys.

Many people with a TB infection may not be sick because their bodies are effectively fighting the bacteria; these people are not contagious. Later, however, they may develop TB disease and become contagious. About 5-10% of people with a TB infection develop the disease sometime during their lifetime. The risk of converting from TB infection to TB disease is higher for people with certain medical conditions such as:

• HIV
• Diabetes mellitus
• Severe kidney disease
• Low body weight
• Certain types of cancer (leukemia, Hodgkin's disease, or cancer of the head and neck)

HIV infection is the most important known risk factor for progression from latent TB infection to TB disease. Progression to TB disease is often rapid among HIV-infected people and can be deadly. In addition, TB outbreaks can rapidly expand in HIV-infected patient groups. There are a number of treatment options for HIV- infected people with either latent TB infection or active TB disease. State and local health departments should be consulted about these treatment options.

[1](https://www.cdc.gov/tb/statistics/reports/2019/national_ data.htm. Accessed 9/21/2021)

How is TB Spread?

TB is spread when a person inhales the TB pathogen, which may be present in the air after an infected person coughs, sneezes, speaks or sings. Depending on room size, ventilation and other factors, the TB pathogen can live in the air and on contaminated objects for a few hours, especially in small places with no fresh air.

Once inhaled, M. tuberculosis bacteria travel to lung alveoli and establish infection. About 2-12 weeks after infection, the person's immune response limits activity, and the infection is detectable. Some bacteria survive and lay dormant for years (latent TB infection, or LTBI).

Symptoms of TB Disease

People with TB infection often have no symptoms and do not feel sick. If the infection advances to TB disease, however, the person's symptoms may include:

• Weight loss
• Fever
• Night sweats
• Weakness

If the TB affects the person's lungs, the common symptoms include a bad cough that lasts 3 weeks or longer, production of sputum, chest pain and coughing up blood. Other symptoms depend on the part of the body affected (**Figure 4-2**).

How Do I Know If I Have TB?

The **tuberculin skin test (TST)**, also called the **Mantoux test**, reveals whether a person is infected with the TB bacteria. This test is performed by injecting a small amount of tuberculin fluid under the skin in the lower part of the arm. The test spot result is checked 48-72 hours later by a health care worker.

TB blood tests measure how the immune system reacts to the bacteria that cause TB. Only one visit is required to draw blood for the test.

A person with latent TB infection:	A person with active TB disease:
Usually has a skin test or blood test indicating TB infection.	Usually has a skin test or blood test indicating TB infection.
Has a normal chest X-ray and negative sputum test.	May have an abnormal chest X-ray or positive sputum smear or culture.
Has TB bacteria in his/her body that are alive but inactive.	Has active TB bacteria in his/her body.
Does not feel sick.	Usually feels sick and may have symptoms such as coughing, fever and weight loss.
Cannot spread TB bacteria to others.	May spread TB bacteria to others.
Needs treatment for latent TB infection to prevent TB disease; however, if exposed and infected by a person with multidrug-resistant TB (MDR TB) or extensively drug-resistant TB (XDR TB), preventive treatment may not be an option.	Needs treatment to treat active TB disease.

Figure 4-2 *The difference between latent TB infection and active TB disease.*

QuantiFERON−TB GOLD In-Tube test (GFT-GIT) and T-SPOT TB test are two Food and Drug Administration approved TB blood tests. Test results generally are available in 24-48 hours.

The TST or a TB blood test is generally recommended for employees who are at risk because of being near people who may have TB, such as those employed in the workplaces listed earlier. Here are some special considerations for TB testing:

- The TB skin test is preferred over TB blood tests for children younger than 5 due to limited data on effectiveness.
- Some people with LTBI have a negative TST reaction when tested years after an infection. This occurs because the initial TST may stimulate (boost) their ability to react. Positive reactions to subsequent TSTs could be misinterpreted as indicating a recent infection.
- Someone who has another disease or illness is more likely to develop TB disease after an exposure and infection. Testing is even more important for someone with a compromised immune system because treatment may need to begin immediately.

- Two-step testing should be used for initial baseline M. tuberculosis testing of those who will be given a TST periodically such as health care workers and nursing care residents (**Table 4-1**). This testing procedure helps to eliminate any confusion over whether an employee was infected previously or at the work site.

A positive skin test or blood test means an infection occurred, but these tests cannot distinguish between TB infection and TB disease. A chest X-ray and a sample of phlegm coughed up from the lungs are often needed to determine whether an infected person has TB disease. People found to have TB disease must be given treatment that involves administration of antibiotics over a 6-12-month period. The treatment is provided to employees by the employer if the TB infection is found to be work related.

Table 4-1. The 2-Step Test

TST Result	Action
No previous test	Do 2-step test
First test positive	Consider TB infected
First test negative	Retest 1-3 weeks after first TST result was read
Second test positive	Consider TB infected
Second test negative	Consider not infected

TB Exposure and Recordkeeping

Like an exposure to a bloodborne pathogen, an exposure to a known TB source should be reported to your employer. Similarly, you have a right to know if you have been exposed. After an exposure, you may be tested for TB, andif you are infected, your employer will make arrangements for appropriate treatment.

Employers must maintain records of employee exposure to TB, TST or TB blood test results and medical examinations. In addition, active TB disease must be reported to public health officials. States vary in their reporting requirements. The OSHA Form 300 log must be used to record both TB infections and TB disease unless there is clear documentation the exposure and subsequent infection or disease occurred outside a work setting.

Treatment of TB

TB infections can be treated, although sometimes the person is not treated if there is little risk of the disease resulting. Factors that influence this decision include the person's age, overall health, lifestyle, occupation, and drug-resistance of the bacterium.

TB disease can be cured by a combination of several different antibiotics generally taken for 6-12 months. The drugs must be taken exactly as prescribed. This is because many bacteria must be killed. Taking several medications will do a better

job of killing all of the bacteria and preventing them from becoming resistant to the medicines. TB bacteria die very slowly. Because it takes several months for the medicine to kill all the TB bacteria, a person must continue to take the medicine until all the TB bacteria are dead, even though he or she may feel better and have no more symptoms of active TB disease.

Influenza

Influenza, or flu, is caused by a virus that infects the respiratory tract (nose, throat, lungs).

Most people who get the flu will not need the medical care of antiviral drugs, and will recover in less than 2 weeks. Some people are likely to get flu complications that can result in being hospitalized and occasionally result in death. Pneumonia, bronchitis, and sinus and ear infections are examples of flu-related complications. The flu can make chronic health problems such as congestive heart failure worse.

Groups of people more likely to develop flu- related complications once infected with the flu include children younger than 5 (especially children younger than 2), adults 65 and older and pregnant women. People with certain medical conditions are more likely to get flu-related complications. These medical conditions include: asthma, chronic lung disease (e.g., chronic obstructive pulmonary disease (COPD), heart disease (e.g., coronary artery disease), blood disorders (e.g., sickle cell disease), endocrine disorders (e.g., diabetes mellitus), kidney or liver disorders and people with a weakened immune system due to disease or medication (e.g., people with cancer or HIV/AIDS).

How Is Influenza Spread?

People with flu can spread it to others up to 6 feet away via airborne transmission. Most experts think the flu viruses are spread mainly by droplets made when people with flu cough, sneeze or talk. These droplets can land in the mouths or noses of nearby people or be inhaled into the lungs. A typical secondary method of transmission involves a person touching a surface or object that has flu virus on it and then touching their own nose or mouth.

The flu is very contagious. Most healthy adults may be able to infect others beginning 1 day before symptoms develop and up to 5-7 days after becoming sick. Children may pass the virus for longer than 7 days. Symptoms start days after the virus enters the body.

Symptoms of the Flu

Symptoms of the flu may include the following:

- Cough
- Runny or stuffy nose
- Thick mucus
- Muscle pain
- Stiffness
- Fatigue
- Headache
- Sore throat
- Shaking, chills
- Fever
- Dehydration
- Difficulty breathing

It is rare for the flu to cause vomiting. If you have vomiting as a symptom, you probably do not have the flu, but you might have gastroenteritis instead. Some people can be infected with the flu virus but have no symptoms. During this time, those people may still spread the virus to others.

Taking Care of Those Infected with Flu

There is no cure for the flu. However, when you or someone in your family gets sick with the flu, you can take certain measures. To prevent exposing others and making symptoms worse, the infected person should stay home. He or she should also:

- Get plenty of rest.
- Drink lots of fluids.
- Avoid alcohol and tobacco.
- Take medications to relieve flu symptoms.
- Call a medical professional if a high fever develops.
- Consider wearing a surgical mask around others.

Only one person should be the caregiver for an infected person. The caregiver should do the following:

- Avoid mingling personal items such as computers, pens, clothes, towels, sheets, blankets, food and eating utensils.

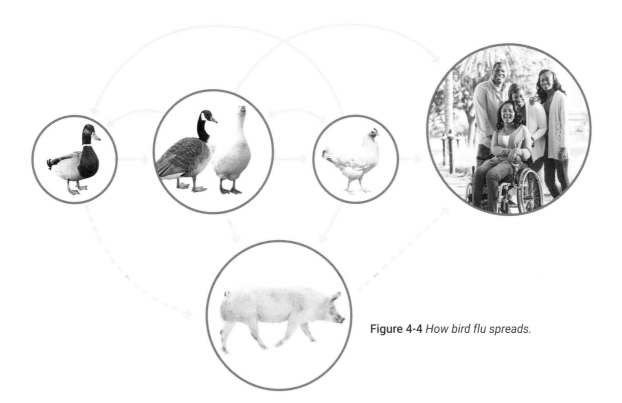

Figure 4-4 *How bird flu spreads.*

- Disinfect door knobs, switches, handles, toys and other surfaces touched around the home or workplace.
- Wash hands frequently.
- Wear disposable gloves when in contact with body fluids.

Everyone's dishes and clothes can be washed together, but detergent and very hot water should be used. Hands should be washed after dirty laundry is handled.

Types of Flu

There are many types of flu. Two common types are seasonal influenza and avian influenza (bird flu).

Seasonal flu is the respiratory illness that occurs every year, usually in the fall and winter. In the United States, influenza season usually begins in October and can last until May.

Most people have some immunity. A vaccine can provide additional immunity. Every region in the world has seasonal flu. However, different regions have different seasons and viruses. Most people recover from seasonal flu, but many people die each year from seasonal flu infection. The number varies depending on the predominant flu virus. According to the CDC, the number of deaths over the past 31 years ranges from 3,000-49,000.[2]

Bird flu infects wild birds and domestic poultry. The degree of pathogenicity varies. Birds naturally carry low-pathogenic flu virus and have mild or no symptoms. But a low- pathogenic virus can mutate and become highly pathogenic. When this happens, it spreads rapidly among birds, and the death rate is high. Bird flu has jumped species to infect humans when they have close contact with birds or their feces or with intermediate hosts like pigs **(Figure 4-4)**. Though rare, humans have also caught bird flu from close contact with other infected humans.

[2](http://www.cdc.gov/flu/about/disease/us_flu-related_deaths. htm Accessed 9/22/21)

COVID-19 (Novel Coronavirus)

COVID-19 (SARS-CoV-2) is an infectious disease caused by a newly discovered coronavirus. It is highly contagious, spread via droplets of saliva or nasal discharge. COVD-19 infection occurs through inhalation of droplets containing the virus.

The COVID-19 virus can live on surfaces for as long as 3 days. Touching surface and then touching mouth, nose, or eyes is a potential route of infection.

COVID-19 Symptoms

People with COVID-19 have had a wide range of symptoms reported – ranging from mild symptoms to severe illness. Symptoms may appear 2-14 days after exposure to the virus. People with these symptoms may have COVID-19:

Symptoms may include:

- Fever or chills
- Cough
- Shortness of breath or difficulty breathing
- Fatigue
- Muscle or body aches
- Headache
- New loss of taste or smell
- Sore throat
- Congestion or runny nose
- Nausea or vomiting
- Diarrhea

Who Is Most at Risk for Serious Illness?

Some segments of the population may be at higher risk of complications and severe illness from COVID-19 infection, including:

- People 65 years and older
- People who live in a nursing home or long-term care facility
- People with underlying medical conditions, such as:
  - Heart conditions
  - Airway or lung conditions
  - Diabetes
  - Morbid obesity
  - Kidney or liver disease
  - Compromised immunity

If You are Sick with COVID-19

If you are sick, you should stay home and separate yourself from others. Contact your doctor or health care provider, as they can help you determine if medical care is necessary. Be sure to take care of yourself, including getting plenty of rest, and staying hydrated. Be sure to avoid public transportation. Finally, be sure to wear a cloth face covering whenever around other people or animals to reduce the possibility of disease transmission.

If you or someone you know is experiencing COVID-19 symptoms AND they have difficulty breathing, persistent chest pain or pressure, sudden confusion, an inability to wake or stay awake, or bluish lips or face, seek emergency medical care immediately by calling 911.

Caring for Someone with COVID-19

If you are caring for someone who is sick with COVID-19:

- Limit contact with the person as much as possible.
- Both the sick person and the caregiver should wear cloth masks. The caregiver should also gloves If they anticipate contact with the victim's blood or other potentially infectious materials.
- Wash your hands frequently, especially after being near the person who is sick.
- Do not share personal items with the person who is sick, including cups, utensils, towels, electronics (such as a TV remote or cell phone).
- Eat in separate rooms whenever possible, and
- Clean and disinfect all surfaces, especially high touch areas, frequently.

Learning Checkpoint 1

1. Infection with an airborne pathogen is more likely for people with certain medical conditions. **True   False**

2. The symptoms of TB disease include fever, night sweats and general weakness. **True   False**

3. A flu shot will protect you from seasonal flu. **True   False**

4. COVID-19 can live on surfaces for as long as one day. **True   False**

5. Who are at a higher risk for serious illness due to COVID-19? (Circle all that apply.)

   a. People who are 65 and older

   b. People who live in a nursing home or long-term care facility

   c. People with underlying medical conditions

   d. People who are vaccinated

6. Which of the following symptoms could indicate that someone has COVID-19? (Circle all that apply.)

   a. Fever or chills

   b. Cough

   c. Shortness of breath or difficulty breathing

   d. New loss of taste or smell

   e. Diarrhea

Administrative, Environmental and Respiratory Controls

Prevention of Airborne Infection

Although it is impossible to eliminate all risk of infection from airborne pathogens in the workplace, the risk can be reduced. CDC guidelines recommend four tiers of controls for preventing the transmission of airborne pathogens in health care facilities. They are:

- Remove the hazard, where feasible, through elimination or substitution
- Environmental controls to prevent the spread and reduce the concentration of droplet nuclei
- Administrative controls to reduce the risk of exposure through an effective infection control program
- Respiratory protection controls to further reduce the risk of exposure in special areas and special circumstances.

Remove the Hazard

The first level of control is to, where feasible, remove the hazard of airborne infection. Steps to do this can include:

- Actively encouraging sick employees to stay home
- Maintaining social distancing, where feasible
- Encouraging vaccination, where feasible

Environmental Controls

Environmental controls work to control the source of infection and dilute and remove contaminated air. Environmental controls remove or inactivate many airborne pathogens. Specific environmental controls include Local exhaust ventilation, general ventilation, and air cleaning methods, including high-efficiency particulate air (HEPA) filtration and ultraviolet germicidal irradiation (UVGI).

Administrative Controls

In the workplace, administrative controls are considered the most important of the control measures. Specific administrative controls that can help address the risk of infection from airborne pathogens include:

• Assigning responsibility for infection control within an organization.
• Working with the health department to conduct risk assessments and develop a written infection control plan, including airborne infection isolation precautions.
• Ensuring timely lab processing and reporting.
• Implementing effective work practices for managing patients (e.g., using airborne infection isolation for TB patients).
• Testing and evaluating workers at risk for TB or for exposure to other airborne pathogens
• Training workers about airborne infection control.
• Ensuring proper cleaning of equipment.
• Using appropriate signage advising cough etiquette and respiratory hygiene.

Respiratory Protection Controls

The final level in the infection control hierarchy is respiratory protection controls. Respiratory protection should be used in settings where administrative and environmental controls will not prevent the inhalation of infectious droplet nuclei. Respiratory controls include:

• Implementing a respiratory protection program.
• Annual training of health care workers in respiratory protection.
• Initial and annual fit testing of health care workers' respiratory protection (**Figure 4-3**).
• Training patients in respiratory hygiene (see the section "Prevention of Flu Infection").

Figure 4-3 *A high-efficiency particulate air (HEPA) mask is used to prevent the spread of TB.*

Preventing Airborne Disease Transmission

Steps you can take to prevent airborne infection include:

1. Immunization (when available)
2. Social distancing
3. Respiratory hygiene
4. Hand hygiene
5. Personal Protective Equipment (PPE)

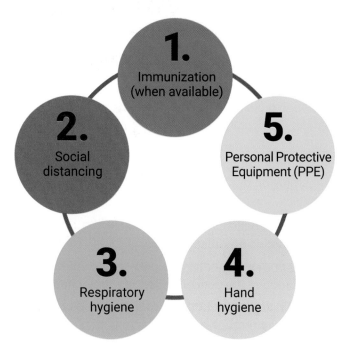

Immunization

Immunization, when available, is a very effective way to prevent infection from airborne pathogens. Annual flu vaccines are very effective in protecting people from seasonal flu. The annual flu vaccine is recommended for everyone 6 months and older.

Vaccines have been developed for COVID-19, as well, and have proven to be very effective in preventing serious illness resulting from COVID-19. Check CDC guidelines for age recommendations for getting a COVID-19 vaccine.

Social Distancing

Social distancing is an effective means of preventing airborne disease transmission. It involves avoiding or limiting time spent in crowded settings, staying away from sick people – maintaining a distance of 6 feet or more from any sick person, staying home if you are sick, and keeping children home if they are sick.

Respiratory Hygiene

Maintaining proper respiratory hygiene is critical in controlling transmission of airborne pathogens. This involves the following:

- Cough or sneeze into a tissue or into upper sleeve
- Dispose of tissues in a waste can
- Avoid touching your eyes, nose or mouth
- Wear a mask when around sick people
- Perform hand hygiene (e.g., hand washing with soap and water, alcohol-based hand rub, or antiseptic handwash) after having contact with respiratory secretions and contaminated objects/materials.

Hand Hygiene

Wash your hands for a minimum of 20 seconds:

- Before preparing or eating food
- After using the bathroom
- After handling garbage
- After touching public items and surfaces
- After blowing your nose, coughing, sneezing
- Before and after tending a sick person
- Before and after treating a wound
- After handling an animal or animal waste
- After changing diapers or cleaning up a child who has used the bathroom
- Before and after using medical examination gloves

Personal Protective Equipment (PPE) for Airborne Pathogens

Examples of **personal protective equipment (PPE)** that can help protect you from airborne pathogens include:

- Gloves
- Eye shields and goggles
- Face masks and face shields
- Respirators

Masks

Masks help prevent the spread of disease from one person to another by blocking large respiratory droplets when a person talks, sneezes or coughs. Wearing them helps those infected with COVID-19 and those without symptoms to prevent spreading disease.

Cloth masks should be worn by people 2 years or older in public. They should not be worn by anyone who is experiencing difficulty breathing, or who cannot remove the mask without assistance, if needed.

N95 Mask (Respirator)

The N95 mask, or respirator is a type of respiratory protection that filters out at least 95% of very small particles (0.3 micron). N95 masks can filter out all types of bacteria, viruses, and fungi.

If You are Sick

To help prevent transmission of airborne infection, remember the following if you are sick:

- Stay home
- Get plenty of rest
- Drink lots of fluids
- Avoid alcohol and tobacco
- Take your medication
- Call your doctor if you have a high fever
- Wear a mask when around other people

Caring for the Sick

If you are caring for someone who is sick:

- Limit contact with the person – one person should give care
- Eat in separate rooms/areas
- Avoid sharing personal items
- Wear gloves and a mask
- Wash your hands frequently
- Clean and disinfect objects touched by the sick
- It is okay to mingle dishes and laundry, but wash them in hot water
- Use a lined trash can

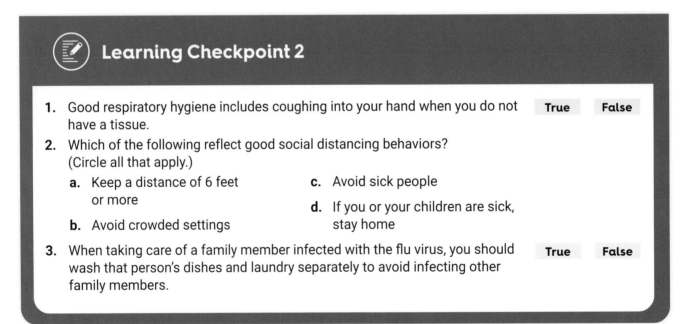

Learning Checkpoint 2

1. Good respiratory hygiene includes coughing into your hand when you do not have a tissue.　　**True**　**False**

2. Which of the following reflect good social distancing behaviors? (Circle all that apply.)
   a. Keep a distance of 6 feet or more
   b. Avoid crowded settings
   c. Avoid sick people
   d. If you or your children are sick, stay home

3. When taking care of a family member infected with the flu virus, you should wash that person's dishes and laundry separately to avoid infecting other family members.　　**True**　**False**

Sample Hepatitis B Vaccine Declination Form

I understand that due to my occupational exposure to blood or other potentially infectious materials I may be at risk of acquiring hepatitis B virus (HBV) infection. I have been given the opportunity to be vaccinated with hepatitis B vaccine, at no charge to myself. However, I decline hepatitis B vaccination at this time. I understand that by declining this vaccine, I continue to be at risk of acquiring hepatitis B, a serious disease. If in the future I continue to have occupational exposure to blood or other potentially infectious materials and I want to be vaccinated with hepatitis B vaccine, I can receive the vaccination series at no charge to me.

Employee:_____

Signature: _____   Date: _____

Supervisor:_____

Signature: _____   Date: _____

Sample Exposure Incident Report Form

Please read this form and the instructions thoroughly before filling out the form. Immediate supervisor should complete this form promptly with employee input. Please print clearly and forward to the Risk Manager.

1. _____   2. _____

    Employee   Immediate Supervisor

3. _____   4. _____

    Date of Incident   Time

5. _____

    Incident Location and Case Number (if applicable)

6. Describe the incident fully (route of exposure, circumstances; describe type of controls in place at time of incident including engineering controls and personal protective equipment worn; identify unsafe conditions and/or actions; relevant police reports).

    _____

    _____

    _____

7. Describe employee's injury (part of the body/type of injury).

    _____

    _____

8. Describe first aid/medical treatment (when and by whom).

    _____

    _____

9. When was the incident reported? _____

    To whom? _____

    If not immediately reported, why? _____

10. List names of witnesses. _____

_____

_____

11. Is the source individual known? Yes_____ No_____

If yes, please provide name/address so that a consent for blood testing can be obtained.

Name: _____

Address: _____

DID THE SOURCE CONSENT TO BLOOD DRAW AND TESTING?

Yes_____ No_____

12. What corrective action was taken or is planned to prevent similar incidents from occurring in the future?

_____

_____

_____

_____

13. Referral to medical evaluator? Yes_____ No_____ Date: _____

If no, explain: _____

NAME OF INVESTIGATOR: _____

TITLE: _____

DATE: _____

(Adapted from The Oregon Occupational Safety & Health Division)

Forms

Sample Sharps Injury Log
(Example 1)

The following information, if known or reasonably available, must be documented within 14 working days of the date on which each exposure incident was reported.

1. Date and time of the exposure incident: _____

2. Date of exposure incident report: _____ Report written by: _____

3. Type and brand of sharp involved: _____

4. Description of exposure incident: _____

   • Job classification of exposed employee: _____

   • Department or work area where the incident occurred: _____

   • Procedure being performed by the exposed employee at the time of the incident:

   _____

   • How the incident occurred: _____

   • Bodypart(s) involved: _____

   • Did the device involved have engineered sharps injury protection? Yes_____ No_____

   • Was engineered sharps injury protection on the sharp involved? Yes_____ No_____

   Comments:_____

   _____

   • Does the exposed employee believe that any controls (e.g., engineering, administrative or work practice) could have prevented the injury? Yes_____ No_____

   Employee's opinion:

   _____

   _____

5. Comments on the exposure incident (e.g., additional relevant factors involved):

   _____

   _____

6. Employee interview summary: _____

7. Picture(s) of the sharp(s) involved (please attach if available).

(Adapted from CAL/OSHA Exposure Control Plan for Bloodborne Pathogens)

Sample Sharps Injury Log
(Example 2)

Establishment/facility name: _____ Year: _____

Date	Case report number	Type of device (e.g., syringe, suture, needle)	Brand name and name of device	Work area where injury occured (e.g., Geriatrics, Lab)	Brief description of how the incident occured (i.e., procedure being performed [disposal, injection, etc.]), body part injured

Retain for 5 years

Sample Exposure Control Plan

Facility name: _____

Date of preparation: _____

We, the management staff of __(name of organization)__, are committed to the prevention of incidents or happenings that result in employee injury and illness and to compliance with the OSHA Bloodborne Pathogens Standard. Through this written Exposure Control Plan, we share assigned responsibility and hereby adopt this Exposure Control Plan as an element of the __(name of organization)__ Safety and Health Program.

A. Purpose

The purposes of this Exposure Control Plan:

1. To eliminate or minimize employee occupational exposure to blood or other body fluids.

2. To identify employees occupationally exposed to blood or other potentially infectious materials (OPIM) in the performance of their regular job duties.

3. To provide employees exposed to blood and OPIM information and training. A copy of this plan is available to all employees during the work shift at __(location)__.

4. To comply with OSHA Bloodborne Pathogens Standard.

B. Exposure determination

(Name of organization) has performed an exposure determination for all common job classifications that may be expected to incur occupational exposures to blood or other potentially infectious materials. This exposure determination is made without regard to use of PPE. The following job classifications may be expected to incur occupational exposures to blood or other potentially infectious materials:

(List job classifications)

_____

_____

The following is a list of job classifications in which some employees may have occupational exposures to blood or OPIM:

Job classification   Task or procedure

_____

_____

_____

C. Compliance methods

   1. Universal precautions

      This organization embraces "universal precautions," which is a method of infection control that requires the employer and employee to assume that all human blood and human body fluids are infected with bloodborne pathogens. Where it is difficult or impossible to identify body fluids, all are to be considered potentially infectious.

   2. Engineering controls and work practices

      The following engineering and work practice controls will be used by all employees to eliminate or minimize occupational exposures at this facility:

      (List all controls necessary and practical to protect employees.)

      Engineering controls

      a. Contaminated disposable sharps will be disposed of...

      b. _____

      c. _____

      (List all procedures used or required to protect employees.)

      Work practice controls

      a. Wash hands with soap and water after...

      _____

      b. Flush eyes and mucous membranes immediately after...

      _____

      c. Eating, drinking and etc. not allowed in...

      _____

   3. Personal protective equipment (PPE)

      The following PPE will be provided at no cost to employees:

      (List required PPE and when used.)

      a. Body protection: (List items and when used.)

      _____

      _____

      b. Gloves and masks: (Indicate when and where used.)

      _____

      _____

c. Eye protection: (List tasks requiring eye protection.)

_____

_____

d. Special PPE:

_____

_____

The (job title) is responsible for ensuring and issuing appropriate, readily accessible PPE, without cost, to employees. Hypoallergenic gloves, glove liners, powderless gloves or similar alternatives shall be readily accessible to employees who are allergic to the gloves normally provided.

All PPE will be removed prior to leaving the work area.

All PPE will be cleaned, laundered and disposed of by the employer at no cost to the employee. PPE, when removed, will be placed in the (designated area) for storage, washing, decontamination and disposal.

4. Housekeeping

This facility will be cleaned and decontaminated according to the following schedule:

Area	Schedule	Cleaner

5. Contaminated laundry

(List organization's procedures.)

Contaminated laundry will be cleaned at _(location)_ .

6. Regulated waste

The following procedures will be followed:

(List organization's procedures.)

7. Hepatitis B vaccine and post-exposure evaluation and follow-up

Hepatitis B vaccination

(Organization's name) will offer the hepatitis B vaccine and vaccination series at no cost to exposed employees. The company will offer post-exposure follow-up at no cost to employees.

The (job title) is in charge of the hepatitis B vaccination program.

(List organization's procedures.)

The (list person or persons) will ensure that all medical evaluations and procedures, including the hepatitis B vaccine and vaccination series and post-exposure follow-up, including prophylaxis, are made available at no charge to the employee at a reasonable place and time, and performed or supervised by a licensed health care professional according to the recommendations of the CDC.

Post-exposure evaluation and follow-up

When an employee has an exposure incident, it will be reported to (job title).

(List organization's procedures.)

Following a reported exposure incident, the exposed employee will immediately receive a confidential medical evaluation including the following elements:

(List medical evaluation elements.)

All employees who incur an exposure incident will be offered post-exposure evaluation and follow-up in accordance with the standard. All post-exposure follow-ups will be performed by (clinic, physician, or department).

Information provided to the health care professional

The (job title) will ensure that the health care professional responsible for the employee's hepatitis B vaccination receives the following:

(List information required.)

Health care professional's written opinion

The (job title) will obtain and provide the employee with a copy of the evaluating health care professional's written opinion within 15 days of the completion of the evaluation.

The health care professional's written opinion for HBV vaccination will be limited to whether HBV is indicated for and has been received by the employee.

The health care professional's written opinion for post-exposure follow-up will be limited to the following information:

(List information.)

8. Labels and signs

The (job title) will ensure biohazard labels are on each container of regulated waste.

(List items that require labeling.)

9. Information and training

The (job title) will ensure that employees are trained prior to initial assignment to tasks in which occupational exposure may occur and that training shall be repeated within 12 months. The training program will be tailored to the education level and language of the employees and will be offered during the normal work shift. The training will be interactive and will contain the following information:

(List information required.)

Additional training will be given to employees when changes of tasks or procedures affect employees' occupational exposure.

10. Recordkeeping

The (job title) is responsible for maintaining medical records as indicated below. These records will be kept (location).

11. Training records

The (job title) is responsible for maintaining the following records. These records will be kept at (location). (List records to be kept.)

Employee records will be made available to the employee.

D. Evaluation and review

(This section recommended)

The (job title or titles) is/are responsible for reviewing this program and its effectiveness (annually or as needed) and for updating it as needed.

Adopted (date), by (highest management official).

(Adapted from the Oregon Occupational Safety & Health Division, based on the OSHA Bloodborne Pathogens Standard.)

Sample Bloodborne Pathogens Training Log

Date of Training: _____

Name of Instructor:_____

Attach:

- Paragraph stating the instructor's qualifications to teach this course

- Photocopy of the "Table of Contents" from the student's NSC Bloodborne & Airborne Pathogens text

Name	Job Classification	Received or told where to review a copy of the Bloodborne Pathogens Standard (check)	Received or told where to review a copy of the Exposure Control Plan (check)

Retain for 3 years.

Index

A

Acquired immunodeficiency syndrome. *See* AIDS

Administrative controls 46

AIDS (acquired immunodeficiency syndrome) 6, 13-15

Airborne pathogens

  definition of 37

  transmission of . . . 6, 37, 38, 44

  types of 37, 44

Alerts

  antiseptic hand cleanser. . . . 26

  contaminated clothing 27

  exposure incident 35

  hand washing. 22

  hepatitis B vaccination 9

  latex allergy 29

  picking up sharps or broken glass. 24

  unknown body fluid 7

Antibiotics 16, 40, 41

Avian influenza. *See* Bird flu

B

Bacterial pathogens 37

Barriers 28-33

Biohazard label. *See* Warning label

Biohazardous waste 20, 26

Bird flu 43

Bloodborne pathogens

  Centers for Disease Control and Prevention (CDC) guidelines . .12

  definition of 1, 6

  transmission of 6

  See also Bloodborne Pathogens Standard

Bloodborne Pathogens Standard

  employees protected under . . 2

  exclusions from 2

  overview 1

  recordkeeping 3, 4

  Sample Bloodborne Pathogens Training Log 59

  training requirements 3

  See also Exposure Control Plan

Blood tests. *See* individual diseases

Blood supply

  safety of 8

Body piercing. 10

Body substance isolation (BSI) 33

Booties 31

C

Caps 31

Caregiver 48

Compromised immune system 10, 40

Contaminated surfaces . . 8, 9, 28

COVID-19

  care for 44

  definition of 44

  prevention of. 44-48

  symptoms of 44

  those at risk 44

  transmission of 44

  vaccination for 47

D

Decontamination. 22

Direct contact 6

E

Ebola hemorrhagic fever 17

Engineering controls

  definition of. 18

  OSHA requirements. . 18, 19, 33

Environmental controls (for TB) 45

Epidemic 38

Exposure Control Plan 35

  Sample Exposure Control Plan 54-58

Exposure factors. 7

Exposure Incident Reporting . . 34

  Sample Incident Reporting Form 50, 51

Eyes, protection for. 31

Eye wash stations 20

F

Face shields and masks. .31, 47, 48

Flu (Influenza)

  care for 42

  cause of 41

  complications of 41, 42

  COVID-19 38

  epidemics and pandemics . . 38

  prevention of infection 46

  symptoms of 42

  transmission of 37, 42

  types of 43

  vaccination for 47

Fungal pathogens (fungus) 3

G

General Duty Clause
(Public Law 91-596) 37
Gloves. 28, 29
Goggles 31
Good Samaritans 3

H

Hand hygiene. 21, 47
   definition of 21
Hand rubs
   benefits of 22
Hand washing
   general guidelines 22
   infection prevention. 47
Health Insurance Portability and
Accountability Act. See HIPAA
Hepatitis A (HAV) 16
Hepatitis B (HBV)
   blood test for 9
   casual contact 9
   prevention of infection 10
   Sample Vaccine Declination
   Form 49
   symptoms of 8
   transmission of 8, 9
   vaccination for 9, 10
Hepatitis C (HCV)
   blood test for 12
   definition of 11
   prevention of infection 12
   symptoms of 12
   transmission of 11
Hepatitis E (HEV) 16
High-efficiency particulate air
(HEPA) 45

HIV (human immunodeficiency
virus)
   blood test for 15
   definition of 13
   prevention of infection 15
   casual contact and 14
   health care workers,
   risk to 13, 14
   risk of TB 39
   symptoms of 14
   transmission of 13, 14
HIPAA (Health Insurance
Portability and Accountability
Act) 4
Human body fluids 6

I

Immune system. 6
Immunization. See Vaccination
Indirect contact 6
Influenza. See Flu
IV drug use. 8-11

L

Labels. See Warning labels
Laundry. 26
Liver disease 8, 9, 11

M

Malaria 17
Mantoux test. See Tuberculin
skin test
Mycobacterium tuberculosis
(M. tuberculosis) 38

N

National Fire Protection
Association (NFPA). 1
Needles (Needlesticks)
   handling of 26
   spreading disease 8, 9, 11
   See also Sharps
Needlestick Safety and
Prevention Act 4
Novel Coronavirus
   See COVID-19

O

Occupational exposure
   OSHA definition of 2
Occupational Exposure to
Bloodborne Pathogens Standard.
See Bloodborne Pathogens
Standard
Occupational Safety and Health
Act of 1970 37
OSHA Form 301 (Injury and
Illness Incident Record) 3, 4
OSHA Form 300 (Injury and
Illness Log) 3, 4, 40
Other potentially infectious
materials (OPIM). 1
   human body fluids and other
   contaminants. 6

P

Pandemics. 38
Pathogens
   definition of 1
Personal protective equipment
(PPE). 28
   disposal of contaminated. . . 32
   improvising. 32

Index

See also Individual items of PPE

Protective body clothing 31

Q

QuantiFERON–TB GOLD In-Tube (QFT-G) blood test 40

R

Recording and Reporting Occupational Injuries and Illnesses (OSHA 29 CFR Part 1904) . . . 3, 4

Regulated waste
   handling and disposal 26

Respiratory hygiene 47

Respiratory protection controls
. . . . 46

S

Safety glasses 31

SARS-CoV-2
   See COVID-19

Sharps
   definition of 29
   handling of 26
   sharps containers 19
   Sample Sharps Injury
   Log 52, 53

Skills
   Cleaning broken sharps and a contaminated spill 22
   Hand washing 23
   Putting on gloves 29
   Removing contaminated gloves 30
   Using a commercial body fluid disposal kit 25

Social distancing 47

Standard precautions 33, 34

Sterilization guidelines 22

Syphilis 16

T

Tattooing 10

T-SPOT TB blood test 40

Tuberculin skin test (TST) 39

Tuberculosis (TB) 37
   active TB disease 39, 40
   incidence of 38
   latent TB infection (LTBI) . . . 39
   prevention of infection . . 39, 40
   required recordkeeping 41
   risk factors for 38, 39
   symptoms of 39
   testing for 39, 40
   transmission of 39
   treatment of 41

Two-step TB testing 41

U

Ultraviolet germicidal irradiation (UVGI) 45

Unexpected exposure
   emergency procedures for 33, 34
   improvising PPE for 32
   Sample Exposure Incident Report Form 50, 51

Universal precautions 33, 34

V

Vaccination
   right to refuse 10

See also Individual diseases

Vector transmission 6

Viral pathogens 37

W

Warning labels
   biohazard label 20
   biohazard symbol 20
   requirements 20

West Nile Virus 17

Work area restrictions 27

Work practice controls 21